1

Multimedia

Production
HANDBOOK

From the idea
to the remake:
Theater, Radio,
Filming,
Television,
Internet and more

COPYRIGHT

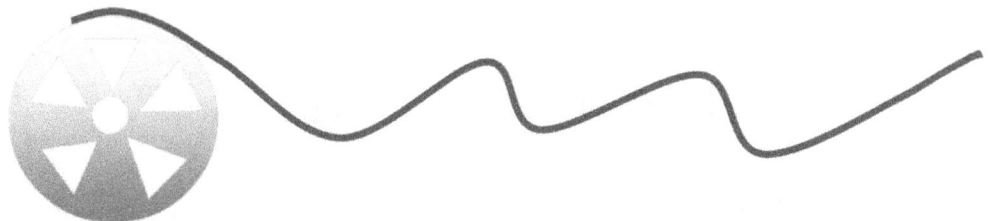

CONTENTS
Multimedia Production Handbook

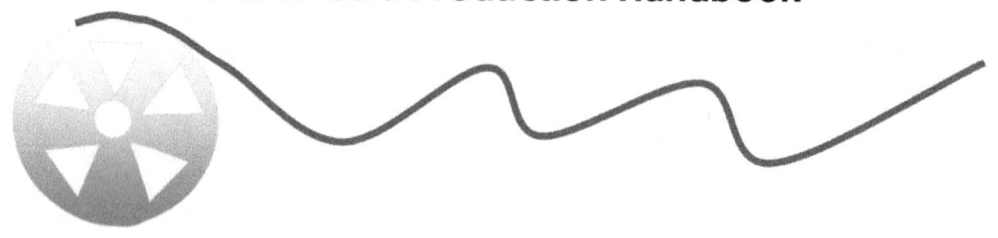

ABOUT THE AUTHOR

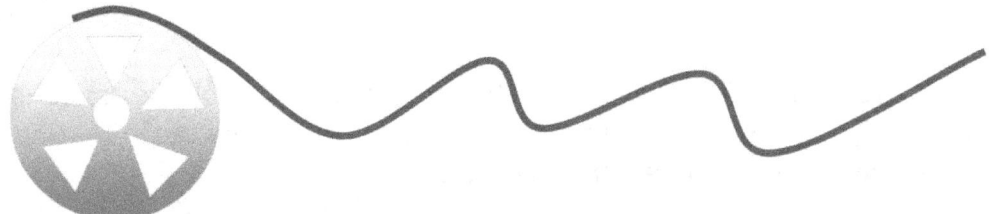

David Isaac Ruiz A. (April 14, 1981), is a Panamanian communicator, writer and screenwriter. He is the author of the monograph for undergraduate degree entitled "50 years of educational television: evolution and rethinking" University of Panama, 2003. Published for the first time stories and poetry in the collective book "To tell is not game", 2007, along with other new authors graduates of the Diploma of Literary Creation taught by the writer Enrique Jaramillo Levi at the Technological University of Panama. During his life Ruiz has also dabbled in the development of film projects such as the animated feature film "El Waca de Plata", which was awarded as a finalist in the Panama Film Lab 2013, and co-author of the script adapted for the feature film of the homonymous novel " Mujeres en fuga "by the Panamanian writer Rose Marie Tapia, 2015. Her knowledge in the science of nutrition, which is exposed in the work" 12 Diets of Fullness "are based on the most recent research and translations compiled from her extensive work in medical journalism since 2009. Another of the digital books published with the collaboration of aesthetic professionals is "Esthetician's Guide: Introduction and practice for Spa and aesthetic clinics" which is focused on health therapies and treatments and most proven beauty today.

Also available on Amazon.com:

· "Jean Santeuil" by Marcel Proust, 1954. A french to spanish novel of historical fiction reedited with cover, reference notes and preface by David Ruiz. (2015)
· "Three Polars Bears at Christmas" by Aaron & David Isaac Ruiz, 2018. Children book with coloring book, based on a original christmas tale.

· "Esthetician's Guide: Introduction and practice for Spa and aesthetic Clinics" 2017. It is focused on health and beauty therapies and treatments.

FOREWORD

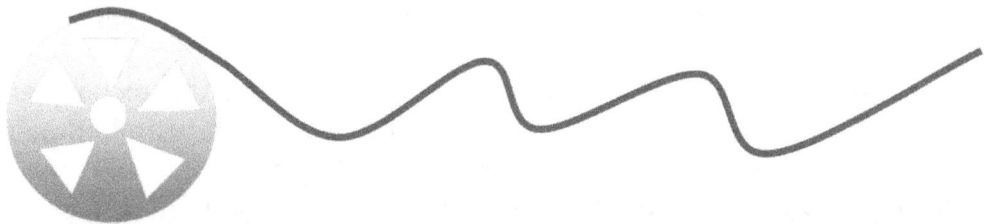

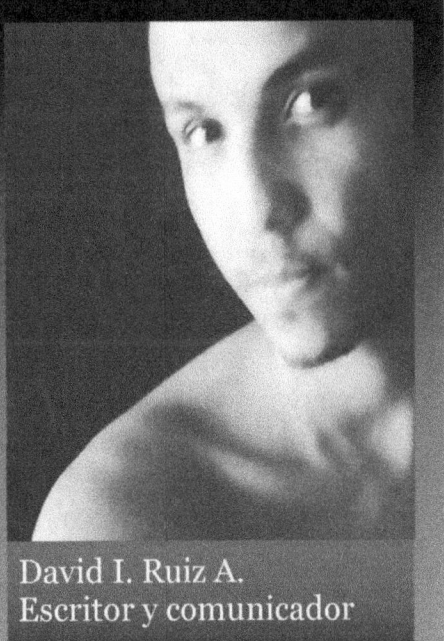

The integration of the text, the moving image and the sound, to translate them into a language that makes them invisible and projects them around the planet has been the achievement of many dreamy inventors.

The future we dream of will depend on how we learn to take advantage of it wisely.

David I. Ruiz A.
Escritor y comunicador

Our main purpose is to continue strengthening the knowledge of readers. Therefore, we decided to edit this electronic book for all those people who see in multimedia production a hobby, a dream, a profession or a career in life. And as the audiovisual production has not stopped evolving, to improve and to surprise the audiences formed by millions of spectators anxious to inform themselves, entertain themselves and transorb ways of life; this book has several chapters that illustrate, defining and explaining many of the concepts and procedures that are necessary to work within the television and audiovisual industry, without leaving behind those primal media that were giving form and character to what today we call multimedia. You can start your own multimedia projects, or even manage a medium company as your own business.

The bibliography available on the Internet about the techniques and production processes most accepted at present, has been updated with this Manual that did not leave anything pending because all the topics and subtopics that will complete any doubt you have and are related to this have been included. field so influential in our days in the global society.

Beginning with chapter one where we approach the history and the origin of the inventions of media from the Industrial Revolution until arriving at our contemporary time where the digital technology has reunited and reduced its size and increased its capacity. In the second chapter entitled "Digital formats" we define their types of digital files and the benefits of using them in combination, as well as commenting on future possibilities.

We will explore in the third chapter, how the genres of theater, moved to the radio, were improved with visual language and joined the htlm language to project through the virtual space of the Internet, creating a whole new industry of entertainment through of video games, social networks and other subgenres for the most varied public.

"Multimedia Spaces" is the title of the fourth chapter that describes those places arranged with the necessary tools for multimedia professionals. We also found some comparisons of what the process was by means of analogous equipments with the recent and almost definitive introduction of the digital age. In all these chapters you will find mailboxes with main ideas to remember and suggested activities as well as for teachers and film students.

"Project Development" is another chapter of this topic that we develop from the conception of the idea, the process of a scriptwriter until reaching the final version of his script, the beginnings of the necessary legal and financial management of this stage and the role of the Producer and many more recommendations on how to start a project on the right foot.

Another of the topics that we have not left out of this book are all the directors involved in the production, including the field Producer, art, costumes and set design, such as lighting, photography techniques, audio and sound advances and music . We discovered the secrets of page to page, storyboarding, teaser and acting coaching. Chapter seven is about Production and Filming divided into more than ten sub topics. Of course we wanted to divide the precise functions also of the director, his assistants and continuists according to the current trends that introduce the Data Manager. In the final part of this chapter we gather a compendium of the most influential authors and theorists in the study of social phenomena fostered by the use of cinema as a means of artistic expression throughout the world.

Finally the eighth chapter we will know how the assembly techniques differ, based expressly on the concepts exposed by the most historical theories whose evolution until our days has allowed it to sustain itself as a source of jobs for the Latin American economies. Lastly, we included in the Post Production stage, some of the secrets of a successful and blockbuster production, with marketing, distribution and management advice after a premiere with its collection and the possibilities of readapting and selling it as a remake.

It will always be a pleasure for me to share with you, my readers, the most important data of the audiovisual and multimedia production that I have been able to compile for this manual or guide, which although it is not extensive, we hope that you do not stay in the I forget and can take advantage of this knowledge for their profession, growth and personal well-being.

The author.

CHAPTER 1

HISTORY OF MULTIMEDIA

- ▶ The Theater
- ▶ The telegraph
- ▶ Photography
- ▶ The telephone
- ▶ The cell phone
- ▶ The cinema
- ▶ The television
- ▶ The Computer
- ▶ The Internet

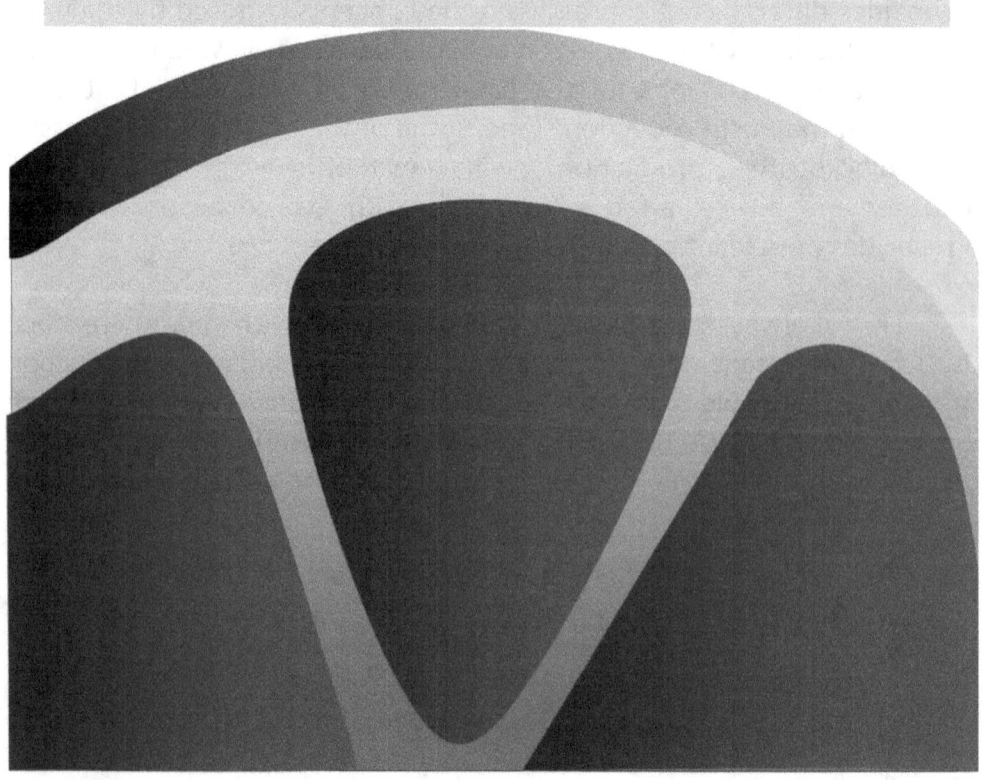

HISTORY OF MULTIMEDIA

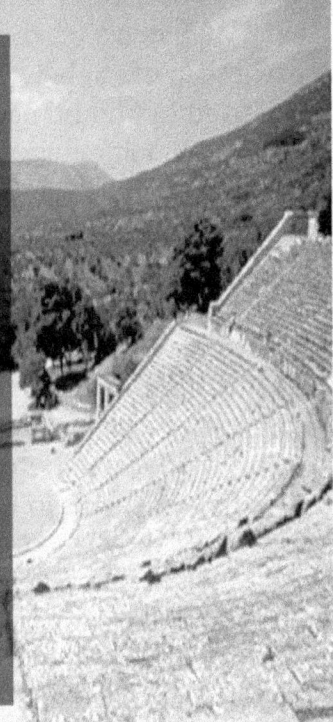

The digital technology of the 21st century continues to bring us advances that facilitate and accelerate our activities as we never imagined before. That obsession of man to communicate at long distances, to influence the masses or in public opinion, to enrich their economies to survive and simply educate and entertain themselves, have driven the discovery and improvement of many machines and inventions since the Revolution have amazed generations throughout the planet. These inventors and their creations marked the history.

From the stone age to computer science, many centuries have passed. If we had continued using the stone, we would not have provided ourselves with the perfection that we demand when carrying out our tasks, as was achieved with the precise materials that make up a microchip, such as silicon. Multimedia is considered as the way to present information that uses a combination of text, sound, images, animation and video. Depending on the device in which the multimedia is played, this can be a desktop PC, a tablet, a laptop, or mobile or cellular device.

Among the most common multimedia computer applications are the Apps, social networks, e-books, games, learning programs and reference material such as encyclopedias on DVD or CD. Most multimedia applications include predefined associations known as hyperlinks, which allow users to move through information more intuitively and interactively.

Multimedia products, well posed, allow the same information to be presented in multiple ways, using chains of associations of ideas similar to those used by the human mind. The connectivity provided by hypertexts means that multimedia programs are not mere static presentations with images and sound, but an infinitely varied and it is an informative interactive experience.

Multimedia applications are computer programs, which are usually stored on external microdisks (SD-CARD, USB or DVD). They can also reside in the World Wide Web (Web pages). The linking of information through hyperlinks is achieved using special computer programs or languages. The computer language used to create Web pages is called HTML (abbreviations in English of HyperText Markup Language). Its latest version is HTML 5.

Multimedia applications usually need more memory and processing capacity than the same information represented exclusively in the form of text. For example, a computer running multimedia applications must have a fast CPU (it is the electronic element of the computer that provides calculation and control capacity). A multimedia computer (it is called that to which it has capacity to execute multimedia applications) needs additional memory to help the CPU to make calculations and allow the representation of complex images on the screen, advanced sound and video cards, speakers and other types of hardware and software that facilitate the execution of audio, video and animations. The computer also needs a high-capacity hard drive to store video and retrieve multimedia information, as well as a disk drive to run applications stored in external storage memories such as DVD, or Blue-Ray.

6th Century BC: The Theater

Multimedia production, as we know it today, is due to the evolution and contribution of many literary genres, but mainly it has been the theater. Naturalism is responsible to a large extent for the appearance of the figure of the modern theatrical director.

Although all the theatrical productions throughout history were organized and unified by an individual, the director's idea to interprets the text, creates a style of action, suggests sets and costumes and gives cohesion to production, is something modern. For a long time, in the history of theater, the role of the director was assumed by the author of the work. In the eighteenth century and part of the nineteenth, the director was often the main actor of the company, the actor-manager. The growing dependence on technical issues, special effects, the desire for historical precision, the appearance of authors who were not directly involved in production and the convenience of interpreting psychological aspects of the character, created the need for a director.

The modern concept of director goes back to the eighteenth century with actor-manager David Garrick, who studied law, but became a wine merchant and finally went from business to theater. He debuted as a professional actor in Ipswich in 1741 with Oroonoko or the royal slave, the work of British playwright Thomas Southerne. Its success took to him to act in London that same year in the paper protagonist of Ricardo III, with which it obtained a sensational triumph. Garrick was equally gifted for tragedy, comedy and farce. He broke with the elaborate French declamatory style, so fashionable at the time, and followed the most natural formula of surrendering to the verse suggested by Shakespeare. As a manager, he incorporated scenic lighting and introduced backdrops painted with naturalist inspiration.

Duke George II of Saxe-Meiningen, who ruled over the actors in his ducal theater in Meiningen (Germany), is considered the first director. The first naturalist director in France was André Antoine, whose little Théâtre Libre produced many new naturalist works. Antoine tried to print realistic details in all his sets and instructed his actors so that they could behave on stage as if they were in any room.

The dramatic art is a literary genre, written either in prose or verse, usually in dialogue, conceived to be represented; the scenic arts cover everything related to the writing of the theatrical work, the interpretation, the production, the costumes and scenarios.

The term drama comes from the Greek word meaning "to do," and for that reason it is usually associated with the idea of action. In general terms, drama is understood as a story that narrates the vital events of a series of characters. As the dramatic adjective indicates, the ideas of conflict, tension, contrast and emotion are associated with drama. A representation consists only of two essential elements: actors and audience. The representation can be mimic or use verbal language. The characters do not have to be human beings; The puppets or the puppet have been much appreciated throughout history, as well as other scenic resources. A representation can be enhanced through costumes, makeup, sets, accessories, lighting, music and special effects. These elements are used to help create an illusion of places, times, different characters, or to emphasize a special quality of representation and differentiate it from everyday experience.

1837: The telegraph

The first electrical equipment for telegraphic transmission was invented by the American Samuel F. B. Morse in 1836, and the following year by the English physicist Charles Wheatstone in collaboration with the engineer Sir William F. Cooke. The basic code, called Morse code, transmitted messages by electrical impulses that circulated through a single cable. Morse's apparatus, which issued the first public telegram in 1844, was in the form of an electric switch. By the pressure of the fingers, it allowed the passage of the current during a determined lapse and then canceled it. The original Morse receiver had an electromagnetically controlled pointer that drew strokes on a paper tape that rotated on a cylinder. The strokes had a length depending on the duration of the electric current that circulated through the cables of the electromagnet and had the appearance of points and stripes.

In the course of the experiments with that instrument, Morse discovered that the signals could only be transmitted correctly at about 32 km. At greater distances, the signals became too weak to register. Morse and his collaborators developed a relay apparatus that could be coupled to the telegraph line about 32 km from the signal station in order to automatically repeat them and send them another 32 km beyond. The relay was formed by a switch driven by an electromagnet.

In quadruplex telegraphy, invented in 1874 by Thomas Edison, two messages were transmitted simultaneously in each direction. In 1915, multiple telegraphy was implemented, which allowed the simultaneous sending of eight or more messages. This and the appearance of the teletype machines, in the mid-1920s, led to the gradual abandonment of the Morse manual telegraphic system of keys and its replacement by wired and wireless wave transmission methods.

At present other inventions such as teletype and fax replaced the utility of the telegraph.

1839: The photograph

The sensitivity to light of certain silver compounds, particularly nitrate and silver chloride, was already known before British scientists Thomas Wedgwood and Humphry Davy began their experiments in the late 18th century to obtain photographic images. They managed to produce pictures of paintings, silhouettes of leaves and human profiles using paper coated with silver chloride. These photos were not permanent, because after exposing them to light, the entire surface of the paper blackened.

It was in the next century when William Talbot created a chemical procedure to get negative images on paper by using a dark camera to make copies. On January 25, 1839 published the details of his method called "photogenic drawing", Talbot discovered that paper coated with silver iodide was more sensitive to light if before its exposure was immersed in a solution of silver nitrate and acid gallic, dissolution that could also be used for the development of paper after exposure. Once the development was finished, the negative image was submerged in sodium thiosulfate or sodium hyposulfite to make it permanent. Eight months before the French painter Louis Jacques Mandé

Daguerre made public the daguerreotype procedure. Both systems consist of immersing the revealed image in a saline solution to fix it and interrupt the development process and make it permanent.

In 1841 he invented the calotype to reveal the image outside the camera. In this method the paper is moistened in an acid solution of silver nitrate, before and after its exposure and before being fixed. It also has the advantage of producing a negative image from which the desired number of copies can be obtained.

In 1851 the British sculptor and amateur photographer Frederick Scott Archer introduced wet glass plates by using collodion instead of albumin as a coating material to bind the light-sensitive compounds. As these negatives had to be exposed and revealed while they were wet, the photographers needed a dark room nearby to prepare the plates before the exhibition, and to reveal them immediately after it. Photographers who worked with the American Mathew B. Brady made thousands of photos of the battlefields during the American War of Independence and used wet collodion negatives and wagons as a camera obscura.

Around 1884 the American inventor George Eastman patented a film consisting of a long strip of paper coated with a sensitive emulsion. In 1889 he made the first flexible and transparent film in the form of strips of cellulose nitrate.

The invention of the film in roll marked the end of the primitive photographic era and the beginning of a period during which thousands of amateur photographers would be interested in the new system.

Since 1950, various trends have been emerging as the distinction between documentary and artistic photography became less clear. Some photographers inclined towards introspective photography while others did towards landscaping or social document.

There is a third tendency, which has developed from the first years of the 1960s, towards a manipulated photography that is increasingly impersonal and abstract. For this, many of the printing systems used in the first years of photography have been resurrected. By opposition, the neo-realist painters have resorted to photos for the realization of many of his paintings.

The work of color photographers is beginning to overcome previous critical prejudices against the use of color in artistic photography.

1876: The telephone

From the age of 18, Alexander Graham Bell had worked on the idea of the transmission of speech. In 1874, while working on a multiple telegraph, he developed the basic ideas of what the telephone would be like. His experiments with his assistant Thomas Watson proved them successfully on March 10, 1876. Especially a demonstration, in 1876 during the Centennial Exposition in Philadelphia (Pennsylvania), he launched his invention to the whole world and led him to organize in 1877 the Bell Telephone Company.

In 1880 France granted Bell the Volta prize, worth 50,000 francs, for his invention. With this money, he founded the Volta Laboratory in the city of Washington, where the same year, he and his partners invented the photophone, which transmits sounds by light rays. Other inventions of his are: the audiometer - used to measure hearing acuityThe basic set of Bell's invention was made up of an emitter, a receiver and a single connecting cable. The transmitter and the receiver were identical and contained a flexible metal diaphragm and a horseshoe shaped magnet inside a coil. The sound waves that struck the diaphragm made it vibrate within the field of the magnet. This vibration induced an electric current in the coil, which varied according to the vibrations of the diaphragm. The current traveled through the cable to the receiver, where it generated fluctuations in the intensity of the magnetic field of the receiver, causing its diaphragm to vibrate and reproduce the original sound.

These teams were able to reproduce the voice, although so weakly that they were little more than a toy. The invention of the carbon telephone transmitter by Emile Berliner constitutes the key in the appearance of the useful telephone. It consists of carbon granules placed between metal sheets called electrodes, one of which is the diaphragm, which transmits pressure variations to said granules. The electrodes conduct the electricity that circulates through the carbon. The pressure variations in turn cause a variation of the electrical resistance of the carbon. A direct current is applied to the electrodes through the line, and the resulting direct current also varies. The fluctuation of this current through the carbon transmitter translates into a greater power than that inherent in the original sound wave. This effect is called amplification, and it has a crucial importance, because until then an electromagnetic transmitter was only able to convert energy, and always produced an electrical energy lower than that contained in the sound wave.

1895: The Cinematographer

Although Thomas Edison had patented the kinetoscope in 1891, the cinema itself was not known until the launch in 1895 by the Louis brothers and Auguste Lumière in Paris, of the cinematograph, capable of showing films on a screen for a large audience. Thus a new mass spectacle appeared, baptized as the seventh art. You just had to add the sound to the images. This was achieved with the invention of sound-image synchronization systems by the Vitaphone (1926) and the Movietone (1931) to be as we know it today.

Louis and Auguste ran, together with his father, a factory of photographic material. On February 13, 1895, they patented what could be considered the first film camera, which also functioned as a projector and a copy printer.

This ingenuity was called Cinematograph, from which the word cinema was derived. It was operated by a crank that allowed intermittent dragging of the film at a speed of 16 images per second.

For the public presentation of the invention, they had the help of the photographer Clément Maurice, who finally chose a small shop located in the basement of the Grand Café on Boulevard des Capuchines. The date chosen for the presentation of the first film in history was on December 28, 1895. The exhibition was attended by some personalities from the Parisian scene, such as Georges Méliès, who immediately perceived the enormous possibilities of what he was contemplating. The program of these first projections was made up of ten 17-meter films, among which were Card games, starring members of the Lumière family, The arrival of the train, which caused great impact among the public, and, above all, Departure of the workers of the Lumière factory, the first film shot by the brothers and an important social document predecessor of the first documentaries.

1904: The Radio

Maxwell's theory referred mainly to light waves; fifteen years later, the German physicist Heinrich Hertz managed to generate such waves electrically. He supplied an electric charge to a capacitor and then short-circuited it by an electric arc.

Italian electrical engineer and inventor Guglielmo Marconi is universally considered the inventor of radio. From 1895 he developed and perfected the cohesor and connected it to a primitive antenna form, with the end connected to the ground. He also improved the spark oscillators connected to rudimentary antennas. The transmitter was modulated by an ordinary telegraph key. The coherer of the receiver operated a telegraphic instrument that basically worked as an amplifier.

In 1896 he managed to transmit signals from a distance of 1.6 km, and registered his first English patent. In 1897, it transmitted signals from the coast to a ship 29 km offshore. Two years later he managed to establish a commercial communication between England and France capable of functioning independently of the weather; at the beginning of 1901 he managed to send signals more than 322 km away, and at the end of that same year he transmitted an entire letter from one side of the Atlantic to the other. In 1902, transatlantic messages were already sent on a regular basis and in 1905 many ships carried radio equipment to communicate with coastal stations. In recognition of his work in the field of wireless telegraphy, in 1909 Marconi shared the Nobel Prize in Physics with the German physicist Karl Ferdinand Braun.

1923: Television

The history of the development of television has been in essence the history of the search for a suitable device to explore images. The first was the so-called Nipkow disc, patented by the German inventor Paul Gottlieb Nipkow in 1884. It was a flat circular disk that was perforated by a series of small holes arranged in a spiral form starting from the center. By rotating the disk in front of the eye, the hole furthest from the center would scan a strip at the top of the image and so on until the entire image was scanned. However, due to its mechanical nature, the Nipkow disc did not work effectively with large sizes and high turning speeds to achieve better definition.

The first really satisfactory devices for capturing images were the iconoscope, described above, which was invented by the Russian-born American physicist Vladimir Kosma Zworykin in 1923, and the tube dissector of images, invented by the American radio engineer Philo Taylor Farnsworth a short time after. In 1926 the Scottish engineer John Logie Baird invented a television system that incorporated infrared rays to capture images in the dark. With the arrival of the tubes, the advances in radio broadcasting and the electronic circuits that occurred in the years after World War I, television systems became a reality.

The first public television broadcasts were made by the BBC in England in 1927 and the CBS and NBC in the United States in 1930. In both cases, mechanical systems were used and the programs were not broadcast on a regular schedule. Programming broadcasts began in England in 1936, and in the United States on April 30, 1939, coinciding with the inauguration of the New York Universal Exposition. The scheduled broadcasts were interrupted during World War II, resuming when it ended.

From the decade of 1970, with the appearance of the television in color, the television sets experienced an enormous growth, which produced changes in the consumption of the leisure of the Spaniards.

1943: The Computer

During World War II (1939-1945), a team of scientists and mathematicians working at Bletchley Park, north of London, created what was considered the first fully electronic digital computer: the Colossus. By December 1943 the Colossus, which incorporated 1,500 valves or vacuum tubes, was already operational. It was used by the team led by Alan Turing to decode encrypted radio messages from the Germans. In 1939 and independently of this project, John Atanasoff and Clifford Berry had already built a prototype electronic machine at Iowa State College (USA).

This prototype and subsequent investigations were conducted anonymously, and were later eclipsed by the development of the electronic Numerical Integrator and Computer (ENIAC) in 1946. The ENIAC, which was demonstrated to be based on Largely in the computer Atanasoff-Berry (in English ABC, Atanasoff-Berry Computer), obtained a patent that expired in 1973, several decades later.

In the late 1950s the use of the transistor in computers marked the advent of smaller, faster and more versatile logic elements than machines with valves allowed. As the transistors use much less energy and have a longer life, their development was due to the birth of more sophisticated machines, which were called computers or second generation computers. The components became smaller, as well as the spaces between them, making the manufacture of the system cheaper.

A program is a sequence of instructions that tell a computer's hardware what operations to perform with the data. The programs can be incorporated into the hardware itself, or they can exist independently in the form of software. Grace Hopper is considered the pioneer in data processing, American math Grace Hopper is credited with creating the first compiler in 1952. Hopper helped develop two computer languages, as well as make computers or computers an attractive element for the world of the company and later of the home with the birth of MS Dos.

1973: The Internet

The origins of the Internet must be sought in a project of the US Department of Defense that sought to obtain a secure communications network that could be maintained even if one of its nodes failed. ARPA was born, a computer network that connected computers located in dispersed sites and operating on different operating systems, in such a way that each computer could be connected to all the others. The protocols that allowed such interconnection were developed in 1973 by the American computer scientist Vinton Cerf and the American engineer Robert Kahn, and are the well-known Internet Protocol (IP) and Transmission Control Protocol (TCP). Out of the strictly military sphere, this incipient Internet (called Arpanet) had a great development in the United States, connecting a large number of universities and research centers. The network was joined by nodes from Europe and the rest of the world, forming what is known as the world wide web (World Wide Web). In 1990 Arpanet ceased to exist.

At the end of 1989, the British computer scientist Timothy Berners-Lee developed the World Wide Web for the European Organization for Nuclear Research, better known as CERN. Its objective was to create a network that would allow the exchange of information among researchers who participated in projects linked to this organization. The objective was achieved by using files that contained information in the form of texts, graphics, sound and videos, as well as links to other files. This hypertext system was the one that led to the extraordinary development of the Internet as a medium through which circulates a large amount of information through which you can navigate using hyperlinks.

World Wide Web (also known as Web or WWW) is a collection of files, which include multimedia information in the form of texts, graphics, sounds and videos, as well as links to other files. The files are identified by a universal resource locator (URL) that specifies the transfer protocol, the Internet address of the machine and the name of the file.

1995: The Cellular

In 1995 there were more than 2.2 million mobile phone users in England and their number has grown since then in all the countries of Europe, until they exceed all expectations. Some important companies in the manufacture of these devices are Vodaphone, Ericsson, Nokia and Motorola. England was the first country to offer personal communication network (PCN) services, which allow these types of telephones to be used at home, at work or in portable form whenever there is network coverage. PCNs operate with a frequency of about 1.8 gigahertz.

Originally the cellular systems were analog, but nowadays they are almost all digital, as is the case with GSM and third generation, and fourth generation 4G mobile telephony.

Cellular technology or cellular radio, is a mobile phone system by radio that has been imposed quickly in many cities and rural networks in countries around the world. The system, a miniature version of the large radio networks, is named after the "cell" units into which a territory is divided. Each cell has a radius of 1.5 to 2.4 km and is equipped with a radio station with its own range of radio frequencies. The same range can be duplicated several times in the same region, as long as the cells that use it are not adjacent. As the mobile phone moves through this mosaic of cells, user calls - identical to those of conventional telephones - are switched from one cell to another by an automated system.

Traditionally, the telephone has been used to transmit the voice, however, it is increasingly used for other types of transmissions. You can transmit images by phone using the fax. Two computers can communicate with each other over the phone using the modem. This type of communication is becoming popular because it allows access to the Internet using simply a modem connected to the telephone line.

Since communications between telephone exchanges is already practically digitized, the future of telephony will include the digitization of the connection between users and exchanges using low-cost optical fibers. The digital signal does not suffer distortion or noise. Using the local optical fiber, the ISDN (Integrated Services Digital Network) will allow direct access to multiple services, such as telephone, videophone, digital television or data communication with a single connector.

KEY IDEAS OF THIS CHAPTER

▶The History of humanity shows us how the inventions and discoveries of several scientists of all parts of the world contributed their knowledge for further improvements.

▶The first prototypes of the telegraph are the beginnings of the keyboard, the press and the chat that we use today, the television allowed the computer monitor and so on consecutively.

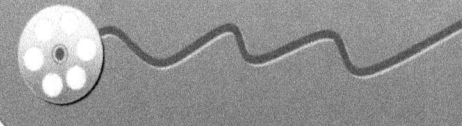

▶The latest advances in technology show that the sale of these patents has created companies multinationals that allow the flow of information and entertainment for 7 billion inhabitants.

SUGGESTED ACTIVITIES 1

Perform an experiment Build a pinhole camera with a cardboard box. You can build a simple camera making a hole in a box. Light passes through this hole and forms in the back from the box an inverted image of the subject. This will be a bit blurry, but with enough detail clarity so that the film, placed properly, give a good picture. However, this kind of photography is only possible if the film does not receive any other light.

CHAPTER 2

MULTIMEDIA DIGITAL FORMATS

- ▶ Text
- ▶ Image
- ▶ Audio
- ▶ Video
- ▶ HTLM
- ▶ Digital storage
- ▶ Digital future

MULTIMEDIA FORMATS

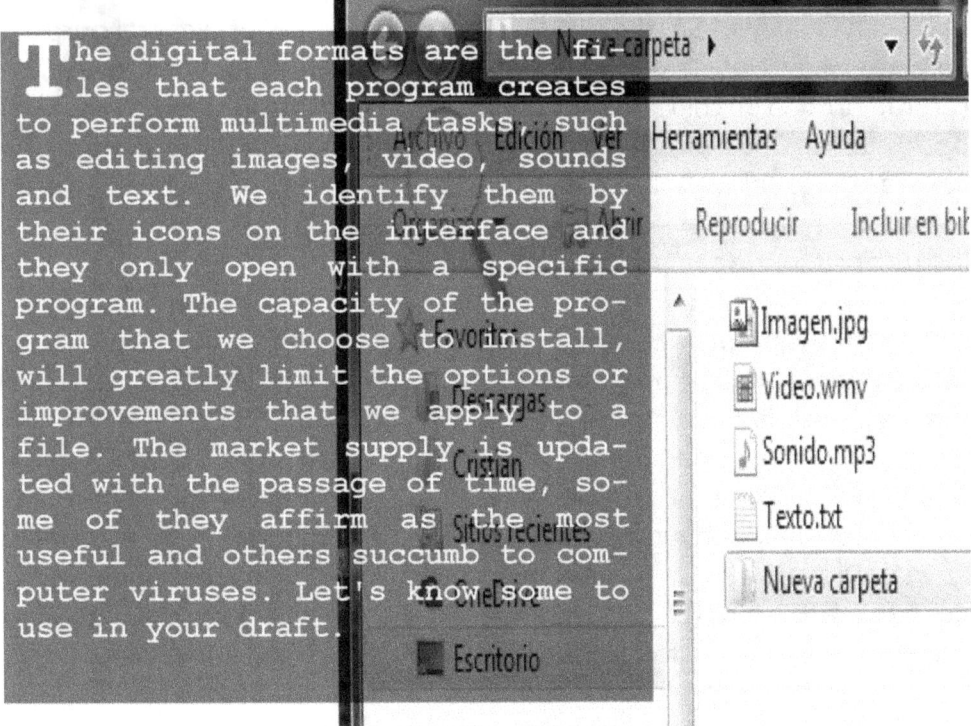

The digital formats are the files that each program creates to perform multimedia tasks, such as editing images, video, sounds and text. We identify them by their icons on the interface and they only open with a specific program. The capacity of the program that we choose to or install, will greatly limit the options or improvements that we apply to a file. The market supply is updated with the passage of time, some of they affirm as the most useful and others succumb to computer viruses. Let's know some to use in your draft.

As we know, all computers first need a previously installed operating system to offer the basic tools to play and edit multimedia files. Any fan knows that these are Windows or Linux, or Mac in the case of the most popular among technology consumers. An operating system is a main control program, permanently stored in memory, that interprets the commands of the user requesting various types of services, such as viewing, printing or copying a data file; presents a list of all the existing files in a directory or executes a certain program.

A program is a sequence of instructions that tell a computer's hardware what operations to perform with the data.

The programs can be incorporated into the hardware itself, or they can exist independently in the form of software.

In some specialized computers the operating instructions are incorporated into the circuit system; among the most common examples are the microcomputers of calculators, wristwatches, car engines and microwave ovens. On the other hand, a universal or general-purpose computer contains some built-in programs (in the ROM) or instructions (on the processor chip), but it depends on external programs to perform useful tasks. Once programmed, you can do as much or as little as the software that controls it at a given moment allows. The most widely used software includes a wide variety of application programs, that is, instructions to the computer about how to perform various tasks.

These output devices allow the user to see the results of calculations or data manipulations of the computer. The most common output device is the display unit (VDU, acronym for Video Display Unit), which consists of a monitor that presents the characters and graphics on a screen similar to the TV. In general, VDUs have a cathode ray tube like any other television, although small and portable computers now use Liquid Crystal Displays (LCD) or electroluminescent. Other common output devices are the printer and the modem. A modem links two computers transforming the digital signals into analog so that the data can be transmitted through telecommunications.

On the other hand we find the input devices that allow the user of the computer to enter data, commands and programs in the CPU. The most common input device is a keyboard similar to that of typewriters. The information entered with it, is transformed by the computer into recognizable models. Other input devices are optical pens, which transmit graphic information from electronic tablets to the computer; joysticks and the mouse or mouse, which converts physical movement into movement within a computer screen; the luminous scanners, which read words or symbols from a printed page and translate them into electronic configurations that the computer can manipulate and store; and speech recognition modules, which convert the spoken word into understandable digital signals for the computer. It is also possible to use storage devices to enter data in the process unit.

In graphic and multimedia design, the most useful data entry devices or files currently are Android phones and tablets, which usually from a USB cable connected to the device allow you to download or copy previously recorded photos and videos with a quality of regular image, not professional but acceptable and compatible for most editors programs, or convertible through other programs such as ATube Catcher to use it in a compatible way. One is the digital camera and the other is the optical pen that are basic and necessary tools for the artist who wants to produce animated short films, stop motion techniques, 2D and 3D, among others.

Below we group the types of file formats or multimedia files that have been best adapted to the programs of the most used operating systems in order to develop audiovisual projects.

Text: from Plain text to Open

Extensions for text files have been modified in recent years precisely to allow users to take advantage of the unification of a single format compatible with all extensions of word processing programs. This is the .odt file extension or Open Document text, which will be the format that will be required to continue converting other old versions such as .doc and .rtf.

Let's briefly review the characteristics of each of these text formats and electronic books according to their extension abbreviation:

•· .odt: Open document text is a format created by the Apache Foundation that allows you to recover files from old versions that could be blocked by updates of recent operating systems.

•· .txt: It is a simple format that works from the Notepad program that lacks some advanced features such as specific fonts, margin, preview, or insertion of images. However, it is useful when cleaning pasted text from htlm sources or web pages.

• .rtf: Rich tetx format is a format that allows you to create documents with advanced features, but of a heavy size to load easily and quickly. For that reason it has been displaced by the format of microsoft windows .doc and later by .docx. However, depending on the results you are looking for, it may be a better option.

• .doc: It is a complex format that works from the Word program, which in its first versions was called Word Perfect. It allows infinity of advanced features such as specific sources, margin, preview, or insertion of images.

However, it is useful when cleaning pasted text from htlm sources or web pages. which was introduced in 1982 as the word processor for the IBM PC. Its ease of use made it spread very quickly, unseating WordStar itself and becoming one of the most popular applications. Both are typical examples of a text mode processor.

• .docx: This is the current version of Word since 2007, which introduced modifications to the .doc format of Word 2013, and which remain valid for its most recent operating systems such as Windows 10, and its suites or drop-down menus for Office, with extension format for .pptx presentations and spreadsheets such as .xlsx.

• .xml: It is another subset of SGML, (acronym for Standard Generalized Markup Language, standard document marking language), which is a page description standard independent of the device, which allows adapting the vision of the document to the size of the document. screen in which it is displayed. This allows the developer to define their own labels; the result is a new format called XHTML, which is expected to be a new formatting standard for Web pages. Its main advantage is that it will allow developing Web pages with different data sets, which could be downloaded to handheld devices, with small screens.

•• .htm / html: HyperText Markup Language acronym, hypertext markup language. In computer science it is the standard format of the documents that circulate in the World Wide Web (WWW); it has been used since 1989.

HTML documents contain two types of information: the one shown on the screen (text, images ...) and the codes (tags or labels), transparent to the user, that indicate how this information should be displayed . To create an HTML document, simply have an ASCII code editor and type the text and labels that are accurate. You can also use specific editors that automatically insert the corresponding labels to the format of the text that is written or to the images that are inserted; almost all current word processors include this possibility.

•• .pdf: It is the acronym of Portable document file of the company Adobe Systems Incorporated. It is based on an image format of each page of the text document that blocks the possibility of editing it, offering security to the reader who wants to store information whose editor program is not readily available.

•• .epub: It is an edition format compatible with basic Htlm code to create electronic books with images, lists, color text, fonts, and table of contents. There are specific editors for this format, free of charge on the Internet, which allow conversion to other formats of devices or readers of electronic books such as Amazon Kindle, Kobo, Sony and Ipad that appeared between 2007 and the present.

•• .azw: It is another specific format for reading electronic books that is based on a security protocol that may or may not block some devices or reader programs, due to its copyright policies, among other compatible or editable features in format epub.

•• .zip: It is the compressed file extension of any specific document or text that allows saving storage space on the local hard disk or as a backup for desktop or laptop computers. Compressing a file inside a .zip folder allows you to save up to 30% of space, however it is necessary to extract the files to be able to edit them again.

•· Other text formats: Other text formats that have been arranged for reading books and other programs or devices, and apps from various operators are .fb2, .lit, .pdb, .rb, .snb, and .tcr.

Image: from gif to 3D

According to the purposes that are sought in the process of editing the image, we can classify the types of images into two groups: vector or pixelated.

• Vector Images:

In graphic design, a vector is an amount that has magnitude, direction and sense at the same time. Vectors are usually represented as oriented rectilinear segments, such as B in the diagram shown below; point O is the origin or point of application of the vector and B is its extreme. The length of the segment is the measure or module of the vector quantity, and its direction is the same as that of the vector. The vector images are in fact heavier and require a capacity of regular disk space, since they allow us to extend them to obtain optimal results for large-scale printing and projection in digital cinema, to say some examples.

The first group are vector images, which are those that are created and saved within a specific image editing program such as Windows Office Publisher, Corel Draw, Adobe Illustrator, and others. These vector images are usually drawings of 2D characters, environments or landscapes, logos, labels, and others. Its main advantage is that its vector nodes can be relocated within the drawing canvas, they can be saved in different format options such as bitmap, jpg, gif, etc .; and they can be reissued in other programs. Their main advantage is that they keep their format raw and without compression or reduction of original data.

• Pixelated images:

A Pixel is in computer science, the phonetic abbreviation of the English concept picture element. It is a point in a rectilinear grid of thousands of points treated individually, to form an image on the computer screen or in the printer. Just as a bit is the smallest unit of information that a computer or computer can process, a pixel is the smallest element that hardware and screen and printer software can manipulate when creating letters, numbers or graphics.

When publishing photographs on a web page or sending them by email, so that the transfer is not excessively long, the weight or Kbytes of the image file is very important, and pixelated images are appropriate. In this case, it is advisable to use formats that use compression.

To print photographs, where the weight of the file is not so important, you can use other formats that offer more quality than those used for web. The same happens when taking photographs with the cameras, the choice of format will be made depending on what you want to obtain and the processes that the photographer wishes to carry out afterwards.

Cameras and digital devices such as tablets and cell phones store the images in .JPE format, while the scanners do them in .TIFF format, in many programs the following types of graphics can be imported:

• Encapsulated PostScript (.eps)

• Graphics exchange format, CompuServe format (.gif or .gfa) Pretty old format developed by Compuserve in order to get very small files. Supports only 256 colors so it is not suitable for photographic images but is very appropriate for logos, drawings, etc. It allows to create animations (animated gif) and transparencies.

• JPEG file exchange format (.jpeg, .jpg, .jfif or .jpe) It is one of the best known and used formats for digital photographs since it supports millions of colors. It is supported by most cameras and scanners and is widely used in web pages, sending photos by email, multimedia presentations and making videos of photographs. JPEG supports different levels of compression, so that more compression, lower quality and smaller files (less Kbytes), less compression, higher quality and larger files (more Kbytes). The compression made by JPEG is lossy and affects the image quality. Every time a JPEG photo is opened and manipulated in a computer, the image when compressed and decompressed is degraded, so it is better not to save them in JPEG if they are to be modified. It is recommended in this case to use TIFF or BMP to edit them and convert them to JPEG at the end. If you have no choice but to edit in JPEG, manipulate them carefully and not excessively.

• Portable network graphics (.png) Format created in order to replace GIF. It uses free compression systems, and supports many more colors than GIF. It also supports transparencies but no animations. By supporting more colors it is possible to create transparent images in greater detail.

• TIFF format (.tif or .tiff) Format used for scanning, editing and printing photo images It is compatible with almost all operating systems and image editors. As a PSD, it supports millions of colors, layers, alpha channels ... and also includes some cameras and most scanners.

• Microsoft Windows Bitmap (.bmp) Format introduced by Microsoft and originally used by the Windows operating system to save your images.

• Windows metafile (.wmf)

• Compressed Windows metafile (.wmz)

• Improved Windows metafile (.emf)

• Improved metafile of compressed Windows (.emz)

• Macintosh PICT (.pct or .pict)

• Compressed Macintosh PICT format (.pcz)

• CorelDraw (.cdr)

• PSD. It is the default format of the Adobe Photoshop image editor and therefore it is a suitable format to edit images with this program and other compatible ones. Supports millions of colors, layers, channels· Graphics metafile for PC (.cgm)

Video: from mp4 to blue ray

Among the oldest forms of video recording and playback known to the audiovisual professional, we observed that it was the Sony company that developed the Betamax system, the first home video recording system on the market, but the video tape format that it used. , the Beta, was superseded by the VHS video tape format, marketed by Radio Corporation of America (RCA). The VHS format has become the standard system within the video tape industry until the 2000s. However, Sony's Betacam system remained the standard system for professional equipment and television stations.

The NTSC, named after the National Television System Committee, is the analogue television system that has been used in North America, Central America, most of South America and Japan among others. A derivative of NTSC is the PAL system that is used in Europe and some countries in South America such as Argentina, Uruguay and Brazil.

The color coding of the NTSC System is used with Television Standard M, which consists of 29.97 frames of video per second with interlaced scanning. Each frame or frame is composed of two fields, each of which consists of 262.5 scan lines, for a total of 525 scan lines, of which 480 make up the visible frame. The rest, during the vertical erase interval, is used for synchronization and vertical return. This interval was originally designed to leave blank the CRT of the first television receivers. However, some of these lines may now contain other data such as subtitles and vertical interval time code (VITC). In the complete plot, the pairs of lines (from 2 to 524) in the first field and the odd lines (from 1 to 525) are drawn in the complete plot (without taking into account the half lines due to the interlace). second field, to provide a flicker-free image at an update frequency of approximately 59.94 Hz (actually, 60 Hz). By way of comparison, 576i systems such as PAL-B / G / N and SECAM use 625 lines, of which 576 are visible, and thus provide a higher vertical resolution, but a temporal resolution of less than 25 frames or 50 fields per second.

The NTSC refresh rate or vertical refresh rate in the black-and-white TV system was originally exactly matched to the nominal frequency of 60 Hz of alternating current used in the United States. The adaptation of the field update rate to the frequency of the electrical energy prevented the intermodulation (or beating) that produces rolling bars on the screen. When the color was added to the television, the refresh rate was slightly reduced to 59.94 Hz to eliminate stationary dot patterns between the frequency difference between the sound and color carriers. The synchronization of the two frequencies, by the way, helped the kinescope cameras to record the first live television broadcasts, since it was very easy to synchronize a film camera to capture a video frame in each frame of the film by means of the use of the frequency of the alternating current to adjust the speed of the synchronous motor of alternating current of the camera. By the time the frame rate changed to 29.97 frames per second for color systems, it was easier to shoot the camera shutter from the video signal itself.

The figure of 525 lines was chosen as a consequence of the limitations of the use of the spectrum. A video signal of 525 lines and 30 frames per second, needs a bandwidth of 6 MHz. In the first practical TV systems, a voltage controlled main oscillator was operated at twice the horizontal line frequency, and this frequency was divided by the number of lines used (in this case 525) to obtain the field frequency (60 Hz). This frequency was then compared to the frequency of the 60 Hz power line and any discrepancy was corrected by adjusting the frequency of the main oscillator. For interlaced scanning, an odd number of lines per frame is required in order to make the vertical return distance identical for even and odd fields, which meant that the frequency of the master oscillator had to be divided by a number odd. At that time, the only practical method of frequency division was the use of a multivibrator vacuum tube chain. The total division ratio is the product of the division relations of the entire chain. Since all the prime factors of an odd number are also odd, it follows that all divisions in the chain also had to divide by odd numbers, and these had to be relatively small, because by harmonic filtering performance is lost. The practice sequence closest to 500 that met these criteria was 3 × 5 × 5 × 7 = 525. For the same reason, in the rules of 625 European lines, CCIR Standard (625 lines 25 frames per second) uses 5 × 5 × 5 × 5; in the old British standard of 405 lines the sequence was 3 × 3 × 3 × 3 × 5 and in the French standard of 819 lines, the 3 × 3 × 7 × 13 ratio was used. The EIA Standards of 525/30 used a 6 MHz bandwidth, the CCIR 625/25 occupied 7 or 8 MHz of bandwidth (depending on the norm of each country), while the French standard 819/25 occupied 10 Mhz.

The original PAL system is PAL-B. It was developed in Germany by Dr. Walter Bruch of the Telefunken company. It basically uses the same principles of the NTSC system, but with the difference that the R-Y color difference signal inverts the 180 ° phase between one line and the next. This inversion allows detecting the phase changes of the color vectors and also allows modulation of the color subcarrier in Vestigial Sideband with suppressed carrier and with the same bandwidth for each signal color difference (which is impossible in the NTSC system, which uses the differential bandwidth between signals I and Q).

When the color television signal transmission systems appeared, the black-and-white system was already widespread and therefore, it was necessary for the color transmission system to be compatible with the existing receivers. The transmission systems B / N are based on the capture by the camera of a luminance signal. In contrast, in color television transmission systems it is necessary to specify the color of an image element by decomposing the three primary colors red (R), green (G) and blue (B). The chosen system to transmit the signal was the combination of the luminance (Y), and two color difference signals R-Y, B-Y. These two difference signals were chosen because they achieve greater protection against interference and noise.

This system meets the basic conditions of compatibility between systems:
• The B / N receivers could reproduce the broadcast signal with color information but in B / N.

• The color receivers could reproduce in B / N the signal of stations that still emit monochromatic signals.

VIDEO RECORDING AND REPRODUCTION: HOME AND COMMERCIAL CURRENT

A video compression format (or a video compression specification) is an implementation to digitally represent a video as a file or a bitstream by means of video compression, necessary for the transmission of data because the large amount of data involved in these applications, they often exceed the hardware processing capabilities of today, despite rapid advances in semiconductors, computers and other related industries. Video compression is a process by which the video image is reduced so that it complies with a required bit rate, while the quality of the reconstructed image satisfies a requirement for an application. This compression seeks to make video transmission more efficient.

In video reproduction, two types of formats are currently used: highly compressed, medium-definition video formats such as .avi, .mp4, WMV, among others. And the formats of little to no video compression, that is raw and without loss of quality, such as MPEG-4 AVC (H.264), HD and Blue Ray.

•.AVI: The AVI (Audio Video Interleaved, audio video interleaved) is a Windows format, which can only be run under this platform.

•.MP4: It is a format of high compatibility of audio and video created for the Web and devices of low resolution, and even diverse operative systems like Windows, Linux and Mac. However its resolution arrives only until 1920x1080 in medium definition, greater than This is considered digital cinema as we explain below.

•.WMV: Windows Media video is another of the exclusive formats of the Microsoft Platform, which allows fans to edit videos, music and text at the same time as adding transition effects and is used through Movie Maker.

•.MOV: It is the QuickTime Movie (MOV), corresponding to the MPEG standard. The QuickTime Movie (MOV) format, created by Apple, is multiplatform and in its most recent versions allows interacting with 3D movies and virtual reality.

•.AIC: It is a format of Mac Platform, so that they recognize other formats since they do not work with them, they recompress it to their own, the "Apple Intermediate Codec", which preserves the quality and improves the speed to work with it at the expense of to increase the size of the files considerably; as an example: 200 MB becomes 2 GB of video.

High resolution digital cinema and video have brought in the last decade; 2010 to the present:

• AVCHD: AVCHD (Advanced Video Coding High Definition) is a high definition video recording and playback format released by Sony and Panasonic in 2006. It can be stored on various storage media, including miniDVD discs (8 cm recordable DVDs) , hard drives, and SD memory cards and Memory Stick Pro, and has been designed to compete with portable camcorder recording formats such as HDV and MiniDV. As the name suggests, MPEG-4 AVC (H.264) video compression is used. This is advertised as a more efficient compression method compared to the MPEG-2 used in HDV camcorders, potentially offering both lower storage requirements and better video quality.

The audio can be encoded in 5.1 AC-3 or 7.1 linear PCM. MPEG-2 is used as the transport stream. Sony ensures that the format has a total storage time in a MiniDVD of about 20 minutes of high definition video using "medium" bitrates. In comparison, current 8 cm discs can store 30 minutes of standard definition MPEG-2 video, and MiniDV tapes can record 60 minutes in both standard definition DV and high definition HDV video. The advertised advantages of the AVCHD over the MiniDV tapes is the real random access, since the time search in AVCHD does not imply a rewind-fast-forward operation. AVCHD random access offers a limited practical utility for advanced users. This format can be exported to Blu-ray and HD DVD discs, but in general it is not directly supported by the players unless it and the camera are from the same manufacturer. Panasonic's high-definition players, for example, allow you to directly play AVCHD (both standard DVD and SD cards) only if the material is recorded with a camera of the same brand. In summary, the AVCHD could be considered as a standard for recording and soon to be edited, but not for reproduction.

• High Definition HD, Full, Ultra HD: HD ready and HD ready 1080p are labels or logos that certify devices capable of processing and playing video in high definition, according to the specifications of the EICTA (European Information, Communications and Consumer Electronics Technology Industry Associations), called DigitalEurope since March 2009. The EICTA introduced these labels as a sign of quality, which allows to differentiate those devices capable of processing and displaying high definition images with at least 720 horizontal image lines (HD ready) or 1080 lines (HD ready 1080p). The term HD ready has been in official use in Europe since January 2005, when EICTA announced the requirements for the label. The use of the HD ready tag (1080p) was approved in August 2007. The term "Full HD" or "full high resolution" had previously been used unofficially to refer to devices that comply with the HD ready 1080p requirements. Devices labeled only with "HD ready" may not show the full resolution of an image obtained from a source in 1080p high definition. Many of these products do not have enough pixels to represent, without interpolation, images at the highest resolution of the current high definition range (1920 × 1080), or even in rarer cases, at the lowest resolution (1280 × 720). This limitation does not affect products certified "HD ready 1080p". It is known as Full-HD at the resolution of 1920x1080 pixels on a television or high-definition screen. This is now the standard in high definition (1920x1080p with 2,073,600 points). 1080p exceeds the common 1080i HDTV by 100%, since the HD only has 1,036,800 points with interlaced scanning.

• Blue Ray Disc: Similar to the DVD (Digital Video Disc) with its storage capacity allows the playback of high resolution video content. Currently, Blu-Ray is the only physical format that has the ability to play video in Full-HD, and there are digital formats such as MKV, Quicktime, MP4 capable of storing digital sequences in high definition.

• Digital Cinema: The standard known as D-Cinema, is a standard format for fully digitized cinema projection for commercial screenings. The D-Cinema standard has been created by the Digital Cinema Initiatives, LLC (DCI) consortium, whose members are the leading Hollywood studios - Walt Disney Pictures, Fox Broadcasting Company, Paramount Pictures, Sony Pictures Entertainment Universal Studios and Warner Bros. Studios. The DCI consortium issued a detailed document on the D-Cinema standard, which is called Digital Cinema System Specifications. In this sense, large screen resolutions have been defined ranging from 8k to 16K. 8K1 can refer to:

• 8K an emerging standard for resolution in digital cinema and computer graphics. The name derives from the horizontal resolution, which is approximately 8000 pixels. 8K UHDV (4320p) used in the digital television industry, which are represented by the horizontal pixel count. 8K represents the horizontal resolution because there are numerous aspect ratios used in films. Thus, while the horizontal resolution remains constant, the vertical depends on the aspect ratio with which the director decides to work. The term 16k refers to a screen resolution that has 15360 horizontal pixels per 8640 vertical pixels, for a total of 132.7 megapixels.1 It has 4 times more pixels than the 8K resolution and 64 times more than the 1080p resolution.

Audio: from mp2 to mp3

The way in which the data of an audio or sound file is stored so that it can be interpreted by the computer or central processor is the audio format. In sound, the resolution is equivalent to the number of bits and samples per second used to represent the information. For example, 11 kHz is a suitable resolution for voice recording, one of 22 kHz corresponds to an audio tape quality and one of 44 kHz is of audio CD quality. Regarding the wave formats, the 8-bit ones offer an audio tape quality and the 16-bit ones an audio CD. Therefore, audio CD players, which offer a high sound quality, normally operate with 16-bit waveform and 44 kHz sampling rate values, although higher resolutions (24 bits and 48 kHz) can be used.).

Basically there are two types of formats: those of WAV type, which store the information of the digital sound wave, and those of the MIDI type, which keep codes, as a musical score, which indicate to the computer how to execute the sound that is wanted play.

WAV formats store any type of sound. They keep samples of the original sound that they then reproduce at a certain speed; they are pure sampling formats. The quality of the sound reproduced will depend on the number of samples taken per unit of time; the higher the quality, the greater the reliability and the greater the amount of space that the file will occupy in memory. The formats called WAV (Waveform audio), AU (Audio files), AIFF (Audio Interchange File Format) and VOC (Creative Voice) belong to this type.

More recently, lossy compression sampling formats, such as MP3, have been established. It is similar to the previous one, but it tries to reduce the space that the file will occupy in the memory by compressing the stored information; for this, avoid storing indistinguishable sounds for the human ear.

Symbolic formats, such as MIDI, store sounds that can be encoded, such as those produced by musical instruments.

They have more possibilities of manipulation than the sampling formats, and the files occupy much less space in memory; on the contrary, they can only reproduce standard sounds, but not the human voice. To this type belong MIDI (Musical Instrument Digital Interface), MOD (Music Modules), created initially for the computer Comodore Amiga and with extensive subsequent development, and its evolutions, such as XM, S3M, IT and others.

More recently formats have been established that allow the transmission of sound in real time; they are designed specifically for the Internet and reproduce the sound at the time they receive it, such as the RA (RealAudio) or MP3 radio. The different sound formats are interchangeable, although with some loss of quality in the information they store.

HTLM: from Htlm 5 to the App

HTML is the acronym for HyperText Markup Language, the language of hypertext marks. Which in computer science is a standard format of the documents that circulate in the World Wide Web (WWW); it has been used since 1989. HTML documents contain two types of information: the one shown on the screen (text, images ...) and the codes (tags or labels), transparent to the user, that indicate how this information should be displayed . To create an HTML document, simply have an ASCII code editor and type the text and labels that are accurate. You can also use specific editors that automatically insert the corresponding labels to the format of the text that is written or to the images that are inserted; almost all current word processors include this possibility.

The HTML language is a subset of SGML (acronym for Standard Generalized Markup Language, standard document marking language), which is a page description standard independent of the device, which allows you to adapt the vision of the document to the size of the screen in the one shown.

In an HTML document there are labels that indicate the attributes of the text (bold, centered ...). Others tell the system how to respond to events generated by the user, for example, that after the user points with the mouse an icon representing a movie, the program that plays video in digital format is executed. The most important label is the one that indicates a link (link), which may contain as a recipient another place in the same document or the URL of another document; The latter may reside in the same place on the Web as the current document or on any other WWW computer. The user "navigates" from document to document by selecting these links with the mouse.

As it has been progressing, different versions of the HTML language have been standardized. Each one of them increases the number of labels, which allows new possibilities for the documents; thus, it has been provided with marks to fill forms (forms) interactively, which allow the user to send the necessary information to make queries in databases, buy or request a service. Other brands allow to improve the presentation of documents, for example, by adding funds, tables of contents or intermittent texts. The HTML 4.0 version is used in combination with XML 1.0, another subset of SGML that allows the developer to define their own tags; the result is a new format called XHTML, which is expected to be a new formatting standard for Web pages. Its main advantage is that it will allow developing Web pages with different data sets, which could be downloaded to handheld devices, with small screens.

The software that allows the user to consult documents on the World Wide Web is called a browser or browser; the best known are Netscape Navigator and Microsoft Internet Explorer. It is responsible for interpreting the labels and showing the document on the screen. The evolution of the different versions of the HTML language has been determined by a parallel development of the browsers, which would allow interpreting the new tags. The advance of one and the other has contributed to the exponential growth experienced by WWW.

Digital storage

Some devices are used for several different purposes. For example, in the past, floppy disks were the first physical spaces to make copies of information, today the CD and Digital DVD can also be used as input devices if they contain information that the computer user wants to use and process. They can also be used as output devices if the user wants to store multimedia files of various sizes in their computer. The read-only memory (ROM) contains crucial information and software that must be permanently available for the operation of the computer, for example the operating system, which directs the actions of the machine from startup to disconnection. ROM is called non-volatile memory because ROM memory chips do not lose their information when the computer is disconnected.

The byte is the unit of information that in Computing consists of 8 bits; in computer processing and storage, the equivalent of a single character, such as a letter, a number or a punctuation mark. Since the byte represents only a small amount of information, the amount of memory and storage of a machine is usually indicated in kilobytes (1,024 bytes), in megabytes (1,048,576 bytes) or in gigabytes (1,024 megabytes). The capacity of any technology device is measured as follows:

1 kilobyte (KB) = 1,024 bytes
1 megabyte (MB) = 1,024 kilobytes
1 gigabyte (GB) = 1,024 Megabytes
1 Terabyte (TB) = 10,487 gigabytes

The most recent storage devices that have been consolidated more manageable than the previous ones for the majority of the consuming public of technologies, are the USB, the external hard disk and the SD cards or memory cards. These work with most digital cameras, cell phones, desktop computers and laptops or laptops.

Digital Future

From the beginning, the main weak point of many formats was due to the fact that very few video editing programs recognized it natively on the computer. It was the great criticism that was made to Sony when it launched the first cameras in 2007, and by 2008 the situation had improved a little, being possible to edit, more or less, the recordings in AVCHD on a PC.

Sony says that its new version of Vegas Pro (the 9) allows you to edit AVCHD on your computer. Of course, only for operating environments with Windows systems. In the case of Mac users, Apple has updated Final Cut Express 4, Final Cut Studio 2 and iMovie '08 so that they recognize the format even though they do not work with it, they recompress it to their own, the "Apple Intermediate Codec", which it preserves the quality and improves the speed to work with it at the cost of considerably increasing the size of the files (200 MB becomes 2 GB of video). In the latest versions of Final Cut Pro, Apple Inc. has introduced the new Codec (Proress LT 4: 2: 2: 0) to work on Final Cut Pro 7.0 which works 6 to 1 (16 GB AVCHD = 96GB Apple ProressLT).

Corel ULEAD Video Studio 11.5 and Pinnacle Studio Plus 11 have also been advertised as compatible (Windows environment). As far as its reproduction, at the moment, Nero 8 Ultra Edition Enhanced or Cyberlink PowerDVD Ultra are the only solutions that are presented as available (Windows only), although in Windows 7 the Windows media Player is able to reproduce said format. All this situation may change in the coming months as Canon, Panasonic, JVC and Sony, among others, are taking models of home camcorders that record in AVCHD format and that should give a definitive boost to compatible programs to edit it.

In summary, for Windows the programs that edit it are:
• Adobe After Effects CS4 onwards - Adobe Systems Incorporated
• Adobe Premiere Pro CS4 - Adobe Systems Incorporated
• Roxio VideoWave
• MAGIX Video deluxe
• Kdenlive
• Edius (Ver.4.54 onwards) Canopus - Thomson Grass Valley
• Vegas Pro 8.0 (Ver.8.0b) Sony Creative Software
• Vegas Movie Studio Platinum 8.0 (Ver.8.0d) Sony Creative Software
• Pinnacle Studio V11 Plus
• Pinnacle Studio 12/12 Ultimate
• Nero 8 (Ver.8.2.8.0) Nero Inc.
• Ulead VideoStudio 11 Plus - Corel Corporation
• Ulead VideoStudio 11 - Corel Corporation
• Ulead DVD MovieFactory 6 - Corel Corporation
• Free AVCHD Converter - Koyotesoft
• Cyberlink PowerDirector 6 - Cyberlink Corp.
• Grass Valley EDIUS

For OS X
• Final Cut Pro X (Ver.10.0.3) Apple Inc.
• iMovie '11 (Ver.9.0.4) Apple Inc.
• Elgato Turbo.264 HD Software

KEY IDEAS OF THIS CHAPTER

▶ Multimedia formats are the key elements to plan, build and publish a project multimedia.

▶ Text formats allow us to take our manuscripts or ideas to paper in a more presentable way, the images enrich that text illustrating in greater detail, the video records actions that escape from our visual capacity, audio communicates concepts to us and the computer language takes all of this to many parts of the space, in seconds.

▶ Technological devices allow us to store this information and its accessories allow us to interact between these despite apparent incompatibility.

SUGGESTED ACTIVITIES

Do a practice. On a computer open a text document that develops a randomly selected topic or preferably. Look for an image that illustrates that theme and insert it into the text. Print your text.

Another suggested activity is to collect images on the Internet on the same subject in common, it can be evolution from a multimedia medium to today. Write sentences about each image and in a video editor, create a Video of images with interleaved texts of each segment of photos.

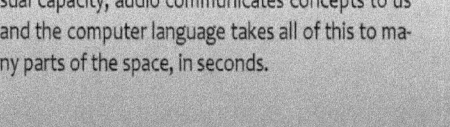

CHAPTER 3

GENRES OF THE MULTIMEDIA

► Theatrical Genres
► Cinematographic Genres
► Radiophonic genres
► Television Genres
► Internet Genres

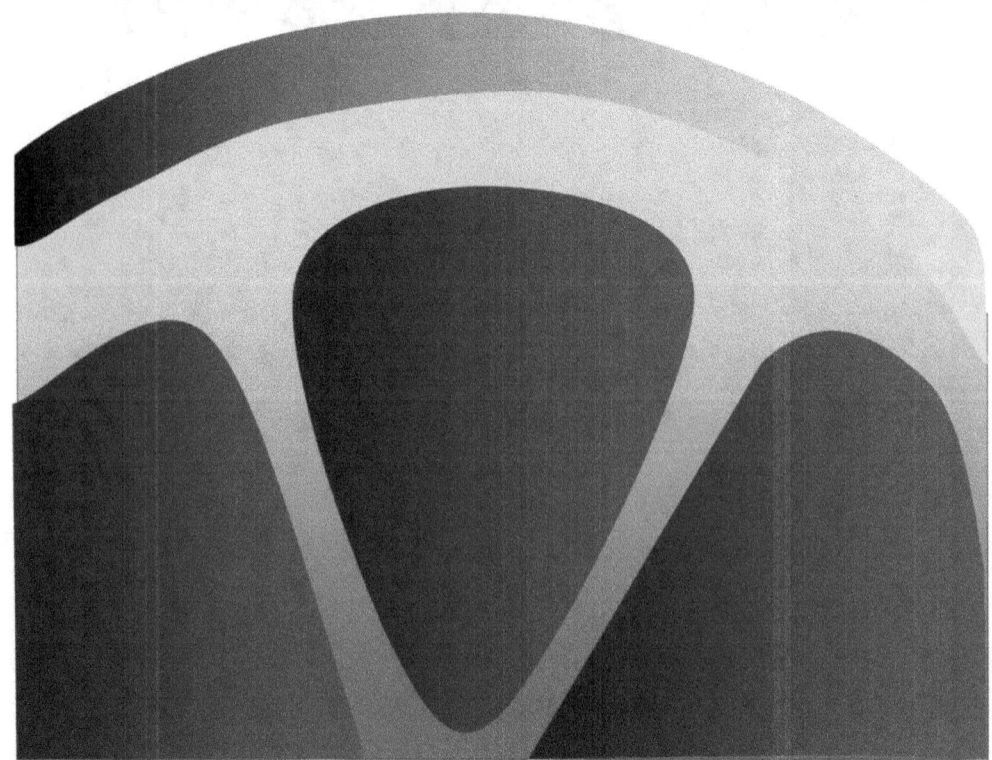

Multimedia Genres

Each means of communication allows us to interact with multimedia tools in a different way. Thus the entertainment experience that is achieved from each one forms a habit in the audience that is capable of remain in your memory, and release tensions through situations, information and other visual elements They capture attention for hours. What was once called the magic of the media, has been broken down into a range of genres that have allowed the development of the mass media that transforms the human thinking.

In classical logic, the genre is always used in combination with the so-called 'specific difference' or own, which makes it possible to particularize the generality of the genre. Plato identified genres as ideas and Aristotle considered gender as a fundamental attribute that can be applied to several entities that maintain differences among themselves.

Scholastic authors developed different classifications of genres and discussed their particularity, following the classifications of Aristotle and Porphyry.

Theatrical Genres

Aristotle argued that the Greek tragedy developed from the dithyramb, choral hymns in honor of the god Dionysus who not only praised him but often told a story. According to tradition, Thespis, the director of a 6th century BC choir, created the drama by separating in a dithyramb the role of the main character from the rest of the chorus: he spoke and the chorus responded. According to Aristotle, from that fact it was only necessary to take a small step towards the evolution of the drama as an independent form with the incorporation of other actors and characters.

The tragedy was born as such in Greece with the works of Thespis and Frical, and was consolidated with the triad of the great tragedians of Greek classicism: Aeschylus, Sophocles and Euripides. Classical tragedies are characterized, according to Aristotle, by generating a catharsis in the viewer.

The characteristics of this theatrical genre of tragedy are:

· It is a serious issue. In general, it is a conflict episode in a person's life, in which life and death are often at stake.

· The protagonists of the tragedy are people worthy of imitation, that is, they represent values of their society. For example, in classical antiquity, they were, in general, noble men, heroes or demigods.

· The objective of the tragedy is to provoke in the spectators two emotions: Fear and compassion.

The comedy originates in the Greek world, but it is developed by the Middle Ages and the modern age, to the present day. The comedy passed between the Greeks by three different states that gave rise to three kinds of comedies: the old, the middle and the new.

The old comedy was a personal satire in which appeared the notable characters, judges, magistrates, literati, with their own names and physiognomies. His most notable representative was Aristophanes. The authority prohibited this kind of representations, and this gave rise to the average comedy, which suppressed the names of the people; but through allegories and other resources the people he ridiculed were made known. A new law also banned this genre from comedy.

Then appeared the new comedy that was limited to the criticism of the customs and the satire of the defects common to all humans. The main author was Meandro. In Rome they cultivated the comedy Plautus and Terence.

Traditionally, there are more than twenty types of comedies defined by different theatrical dictionaries.

The comedy can be:

a- Character: The characters in this comedy are stereotypes, caricatures that are part of a plot that has a satirical intention. It portrays a certain kind of morality to the living: the miser, the hypocrite, the liar, etc. Ex: "The suspicious truth", by Ruiz de Alarcón.

b- Customs: Presents habits, prejudice, fashions, etc. The society in which the author lives. Ex: "The yes of the girls" by Leandro de Moratín.

c- Of ideas: Also called philosophical, is the one that deals with issues and conflicts in which philosophical theories are posed and vital attitudes ... Good part of the theater of the absurd (that used a mordacious humor to give course to its pessimistic vision of the world) could be framed in the sort. Some authors: Calderón De La Barca, Luigui Pirandello, Bernard Shaw, Jean Paul Sartre, Samuel Beckett.

d- Of intrigue: is characterized by the complexity of the action that gives scope for comical situations and surprising and unexpected effects. Ex: "Disdain with disdain", Moreto.

The characteristics of the comedy are:

· Comedy presents inferior beings, that is, beings that embody a vice. The way to represent them is through funny, funny or ridiculous situations.

· The characters are usually archetypes, that is, characters that represent a characteristic feature of human beings in general, such as the miser, liar, rogue, in love, the Don Juan, the swindler, etc.

· Its objective is to provoke laughter in the spectators, but not for free, but leading them to reflection.

· About the conflict that is exposed and that is shown as something that can happen in real life.

· The outcome tends to provoke some kind of agreement that benefits everyone.

The drama corresponds to the combination between the two previous genres, that's why it is also known as tragicomedy. The drama reproduces life more perfectly than tragedy and comedy, because it embraces tragic, vulgar and comical.

The drama itself is a modern composition. He had his predecessors in the Greek satirical drama The Cyclops, by Euripides, and in Sakuntala by the Hindu Kalidasa. The English called tragedies to historical tragedies; theSpaniards, to the dramas they called comedies, although they only had comedy the name (life is dream). He Romantic drama begins weakly with "The Conspiracy of Venice" (1834), by Martínez de la Roza, and reaches its climax with "Don Alvaro" (1835), by the Duke of Rivas, "El Trovador" (1836), by García Gutiérrez, and "Los Lovers of Teruel "(1837), by Hartzenbusch, closing the cycle with" Don Juan Tenorio "(1844), De Zorrilla.

54

After romantic fervor, modern drama is born, a kind of fusion of romantic drama with classical tragedy.

A theatrical drama should be characterized by the following:
· Presents human beings as they are, that is, superior and inferior beings no longer appear.
· In these works man is master of his destiny. For this reason he must cope with his "humanity", that is,
· With its imperfections and limitations.
· The conflict poses situations in which the tragic and the comic mix. It raises individual or social situations in relation to the problems that afflict the man of the time.
· The outcome can be happy or unhappy.

The drama can be:

a) Psychological: paints the inner struggles of the soul and the desenvovimiento of strong passions. Ex: "La estrella de sevilla", by Lope de Vega.

b) Philosophical: it raises the great problems of human destiny, embodying its characters, not individuals, but collective humanity. Eg "Life is a dream", by Calderón de la Barca.

c) Social: presents the aspect of the society of an era, analyzing ideas or customs. Eg "Fuente Ovejuna", by Lope de Vega; "The Mayor of Zalamea", by Calderón de la Barca.

d) Historical: relive a past era, by representing its great events or simply society or customs. Eg "The prudence of women", by Tirso de Molina.

e) Legendary: it is based on legends or traditions. Ex. "El burlador de Sevilla", by Tirso de Molina; "El caballero de Olmedo", by Lope de Vega.

Other theatrical genres:

a) The opera or lyric drama: it is a musical drama entirely sung by the actors, being able to adopt the tragic or comic modality. The literary part is called libretto and the musical part, score. Eg "Parsifal", by Wagner; "Margarita, la tornera", by Chapí.

b) Zarzuela: it is a short dramatic piece of festive character, in which they alter the song and the recitation or declamation. Eg "El laurel de Apolo", by Calderón de la Barca; "Captain Grant's nephews."

c) Sainete: is a dramatic composition of an act, which portrays popular customs and types, in order to provoke laughter. Eg "The trail in the morning", "The chopped chestnuts", by Ramón de la Cruz; "Fans and tambourines", "The piropos", by the Alvares Quinteros brothers.

d) The entremés: it is a brief jocular act of a popular affair, which is represented in the intermissions of the main work. Eg "The altarpiece of wonders" by Cervantes; "El soldadillo", by Lope de Vega; "El guardainfante", "El borracho" by Quiñones de Benavente.

e) The step: it is a short comic piece, of three or four characters, that paints happy pictures of human life.

Eg The main author was Lope de Rueda with "The olives", "The land of Jauja", etc.

f) The Loa: was a short piece that was represented at the beginning of a function, in which the person celebrated was praised or the plot of the work was described or the merit of the actors was emphasized.

g) The Sacramental Auto: they are symbolic representations of the Holy Eucharist. They are purely Spanish creations, which were represented on Corpus Christi day in all the cities of Spain. The sacramental self takes its arguments from the Old and New Testaments, from sacred and profane history. It consists of a single act and several paintings. The decorations were installed in cars, which came to have two or more floors. One of his figures was Calderón, who composed so many and such great works, that he was called the Eucharistic poet. Eg "The great theater of the world", "The dinner of Baltasar", "The ship of the merchant", Calderón; El Colmenero divino ", by Tirso de Molina;" La reaga "by Lope de Vega.

Cinematographic Genres

Currently there is no consensus regarding film genres and there is a complex series of classifications. The film genre is the general theme of a film that is used for its classification.

The cinematographic genres, like the genres of other artistic fields, have their origin in classical culture. The two older Greek genres: comedy and tragedy; one of light style, apparently superficial and happy ending theme, and the other affected, deep and sad outcome. These genres were diversified in the theater, and the first feature films tried to imitate them. However, the possibilities of the cinema completely separated it from the traditional genres, creating new genres characterized by the scarce complexity of its regulation.

It is very important to point out that in the first decades of cinema, the genre of films was corseted, with very delimited characteristics that helped the viewer to quickly understand the film.

However, approximately after the Second World War the genres began to mix creating diverse productions and strange specimens.

The film genres are classified according to the common elements of the films they cover, originally according to their formal aspects: rhythm, style or tone and, above all, the feeling they seek to provoke in the viewer and adjustment. Alternatively, the cinematographic genres are defined by their setting or by their format. The following genera are often specified to form subgenres, and can also be combined to form hybrid genera.

• The color receivers could reproduce in B / N the signal of stations that still emit monochromatic signals.

The examples mentioned in this table are the films whose directors are considered the pioneers in each cinematographic genre in the 20th century. Additionally, there are other sub categories within the genre of action such as narco-genre, western, war, police, samurai and martial arts. In drama we also distinguish other sub categories such as: road movie, catastrophe, adolescents and costumbrista. While the Terror is divided into sub categories: thriller, bizarre or gore, slasher or assassins, monsters and zombies. The comedies are also subcategorized: as the parody or spoof movie, the black comedy and the romantic comedy.

FILM GENRES		
STYLE AND TONE	DESCRIPTION	PREMIERE FILMS
DRAMA	In the cinema, it is the films that focus mainly on the development of a conflict between protagonists, or the protagonist with his environment or with himself.	"Titanic", USA, 1997.
COMEDY	Films made with the intention of provoking humor, entertainment and / or laughter in the viewer.	"Ahí está el detalle", México, 1940.
ACTION	Film whose argument implies a moral interaction between "good" and "evil" brought to an end by the violence or physical force.	"La Máscara del Zorro", España, 1998.
SCIENCE FICTION	It is based on a near or very distant future, where it is possible to see the advance of technology and how this is executed in history.	"Stars War", USA, 1977.
FANTASY	Magic and mythological animals or events without a logical explanation are part of this world where reality is combined with the past.	"Chronicles of Narnia", USA,
TERROR	Films made with the intention of provoking tension, fear and / or fright in the audience with elements such as ghosts, corpses, etc.	"Nosferatu, the vampire", USA, 1922.
ROMANCE	Movies where protagonist couples emphasize the elements of love and romantics.	"Gone with the Wind", USA, 1939.
MUSICAL	Films that contain interruptions in their development, to give a short break through a musical fragment sung or accompanied by a choreography.	"The Wizard of Oz", USA, 1939.
SUSPENSE	Films made with the intention of provoking tension in the spectator. He also usually use the word thriller to designate films of this type, although there are subtle differences.	"Psicosis", USA, 1960.
AVENTURE	Movies where the character moves through places and exotic places wrapped in a conflict related to cultures, races and treasures.	"In search of the lost Ark", USA, 1981.

The examples mentioned in this table are the films whose directors are considered the pioneers in each cinematographic genre in the 20th century. Additionally, there are other sub categories within the genre of action such as narco-genre, western, war, police, samurai and martial arts. In drama we also distinguish other sub categories such as: road movie, catastrophe, adolescents and costumbrista.

While the Terror is divided into sub categories: thriller, bizarre or gore, slasher or assassins, monsters and zombies. The comedies are also subcategorized: as the parody or spoof movie, the black comedy and the romantic comedy.

Radiophonic genres

Radio is the medium in which some genres of classical journalism reach their maximum expression. An example is the interview, the debate and the gathering. The adaptation of the journalistic genres to the radio is characterized by the expressive richness and the personal character that is incorporated into the transmitted message. The keys to a good communication are concise, clear and direct contents. In this way there will be a greater effect of attraction on the audience.

The radio genres could be classified as follows: the report, the chronicle, the critique, the commentary, the editorial, the interview, the gathering, the debate, the wedge, and sportcast.

• The Radial Magazine is a variety program that draws on various informative segments such as health, fashion, entertainment, politics, science, with musical successes such as curtains, with a number of speakers who interview a particular professional.

• The story is a journalistic genre that consists of the narration of events that may be current or be timeless. In this genre, it is explained with words, images, and from a current perspective, and events of public interest.

- The chronicle is a literary work that tells historical facts in chronological order. In a chronicle the events are narrated according to the temporal order in which they occurred, often by eyewitnesses or contemporaries, either first or third person.

- Chronic is understood as the detailed history of a country, a locality, a time or a man, or a event in general, written by an eyewitness or by a contemporary who has registered without comment all the details you have seen, and even all those that have been transmitted to you.

- Criticism is the reaction or the personal opinion and / or analyzed before a topic, several opinions can form a

- Sometimes also a criticism, as long as it is of the same tendency. Criticism is the art of judging the qualities (goodness, truth, beauty ...) of things.

There are three types of criticism: positive, negative and constructive.

- The commentary is a writing that serves as an explanation of a work so that its meaning is understood more easily.

- The editorial is a journalistic genre, consisting of an unsigned text that explains, evaluates and judges a newsworthy event of special importance. It is a collective opinion, an institutional judgment formulated in concordance with the ideological line of the medium.

- The gathering is a meeting, informal and periodic, of people interested in a topic or a specific branch of art or science, to discuss, inform or share ideas and opinions. Usually the meeting takes place in a café or cafeteria, and people from the intellectual area usually participate in them. It is a custom of Spanish origin and remained rooted until the mid-twentieth century in the independent colonies of the Spanish empire. The attendees are called participants or tertullians.

• The Debate: It is a technique of oral communication where a topic and a problem is exposed. There are members, a moderator, a secretary and an audience that participates. No solutions are provided only arguments are set. The condition of a debate occurs in the different point of view held by two or more antagonistic positions around an issue or problem. It is an argumentative text in which the arguments that support the thesis in conflict are intertwined. The arguments must be built in close relationship with the opponent, so the debate is an argument of great difficulty and mental speed.

• Radial wedge is a radio form in which a message is transmitted without presenting itself, but is integrated into other formats, being clear with its content.

For example, a report within a chronicle as an illustration of a round table or a commercial after a song in a radio broadcast. In principle it should not last longer than two minutes and is usually the most common way to introduce advertising in a radio medium.

Television Genres

The three basic forms of television programs are fiction, non-fiction and live programs. The fiction programs are mainly desktop series, situation comedies, drama series and television movies, including mini-series (a film in several parts).

The most common non-fiction programs are contests, debates, newscasts and magazines (informative spaces that feed on varied news within a format that seeks entertainment).

Live television is generally limited to sports, award ceremonies, news coverage on newscasts and some daily spaces for testimonials or debates.

We could summarize the most influential television genres in the last decade of the audiences in America, with the following list of concepts.

▶ TELEVISION FICTION

Serial television: They refer to serialized programs within a period of 12 to 60 episodes, transmitted weekdays or weekend, based on a drama regularly shot in a studio and part outdoors. The themes are varied and are part of the programming of cable channels.

Series of cartoons: They refer to 2d or 3d animations of a unit or serial duration where the character is subject to the qualities of the public. Violence is restricted, foul language, among others.

Television comedy: They are mostly written for adult audiences of trained opinion, since malice or argument delay is often used in the insinuation of situations, sometimes complex. However, the language is also moderated to the young audience.

Soap opera: Serials that emphasize the melodrama or the repetition of situations and love conflicts, with a certain exaggeration of the passions. They are written for a varied audience, although they are usually adults, as housewives. They were exclusive of countries like Mexico, USA, Argentina and Colombia; but they are already produced by countries around the world.

Police Soap opera: They are a new trend for which many production companies have opted to leave the tradition of melodrama, opening up to the male public that prefers arguments more associated with the social and economic reality of Latin American peoples.

Science fiction series: They are typical of Anglo-Saxon and European markets, where serials recorded in interior studios and green screens, surrealist or futuristic ambient shows.

Anthology series: Serial reports on a research topic, historical or cultural value such as reading clubs, reviews of painters, plays, dance groups and interviews with notable personalities of the folkloric field are also expressions that each country should promote through this type of programs.

▶ NO TELEVISION FICTION

Television Contests: Program where participants go through very varied physical or knowledge tests, where through contests, they get cash prizes or valuable items, upon presentation to casting calls, where producers approve a specific plan that addresses preproduction, shooting in studio and editing or even live broadcast.

Dating shows: Programs where single participants find the opportunity to meet and make friends with other singles of the opposite sex. This format tends to mark a good margin of audience so we can currently find it combined with other formats such as reality show, competition and physical resistance, nightlife, comedy, etc.

Reality shows: As the name says, they are programs based on the reality of people, where only some objectives are fulfilled, without action or acting representation of the truth of the lives of those involved. There are many sub categories of this so-called reality TV, as a union of families, locked couples, couples online, etc.

Talent shows: These are programs where the public participates before a jury of professionals, which decides whether talent; be it singing, dancing, choreography, humor or other; they are worthy to receive the prize or to pass to an eliminatory stage of finalists.

Magacín: This is a program very similar to its radial version with interviews, games, reports, health tips, mini competitions, which imitates the magazines in their structured content in blocks.

Medical drama: These are reports taken from patients in their daily lives where they face difficult medical diagnoses, where between each chapter their medical evolution is observed. Some of these are also based on patients of plastic surgeons who correct aesthetic defects before the camera lens.

Supernatural drama: Paranormal events have also been reported through the recreation of programs where recordings made in haunted houses are analyzed, based on the testimony of its inhabitants.

Journalistic Interview: Also known in the Anglo market as Talk show and Late night shows are interview programs for artists, politicians, and actors where they intend to know their lives in depth.

Anime: The Japanese series have achieved over the years to place some successful animes or comics in series format that even adapt to multi-media video games, as was the recent case of Pokemon Go.

Procedural Police: The detective cases between couples and the trials of procedural cause have also been taken to the screen as a reality show, or filmed in studies under the permissions of those involved and in the opinion of a judge.

Variety show: The concert programs, combined with competitions where the participants are celebrities were a unique style that has been modified by the need to diversify the old stereotypes in television production.

Comedy and hidden camera: The Telecomedia is a type of program that seeks above all to make its viewers laugh, and to achieve it many ways are used such as humor, parody, surprise situations outdoors and others.

Telegarbage: The bloopers or errors out of scene are also a material that the producers take advantage of. The homemade recordings and the challenges of adolescence, funny videos and others find their place in this kind of jocular content.

► HYBRIDS AND OTHERS:

Docudramas: Documentaries for television, that is, filmed with video cameras not as demanding as the 35mm film, Docu-reality has allowed the presentation of special programs that due to their actuality, influence on societies and interests are located within of journalism.

National chain: The state television channels have the primary purpose of informing their citizens of the events and decisions that State issues are going to take, in order to consider public opinion and estimate the adverse effects they can cause.

Deferred program: Another of the programs that are governed by state, non-commercial channels, is to indicate by law or decrees the obligations to transmit content of interest to the population. It refers to the transmission from a mother antenna through other terminals that cover the entire territory.

Electoral Strip: During the government elections the television stations have included in recent years strips related to the vicissitudes between politicians or candidates that are the focus of attention for voters.

Infomercial: Finally the advertising spaces have included the option of the informacials, which are the longest paid spaces for companies to publicize their events, products and services in a corporate way in the business field.

Web Genres

Multimedia has allowed, not only the big brands and media companies, but also the entrepreneur or ordinary citizen; create personal content and attract followers interested in continuing to enjoy them, in a free way. These virtual communities have been consolidated to allow advertisers to find consumers for their campaigns, thereby expanding the possibilities of influencing their purchasing decisions.

A video hosting service allows individuals to upload video clips to an Internet website. The video host will store the video on one of its servers, and will show the individual different types of code to allow others to watch your video. The website is called a video hosting website or a video distribution website. Among the virtual language formats that are used as genres on the Internet are the website, the web series, the video game, the music video, the video blog, and others.

Website

A web page, or electronic page, digital page, or cyberpage12 is a document or electronic information capable of containing text, sound, video, programs, links, images, and many other things, adapted for the so-called World Wide Web (WWW) and which can be accessed through a web browser. This information is usually in HTML or XHTML format, and can provide access to other web pages through hypertext links. Frequently they also include other resources such as cascading style sheets, scripts, digital images, among others.

Web series

A webseries or web series is a series created to be distributed through the Internet, and is part of the new and emerging medium called web television. They use scripts and are structured in seasons divided into episodes, which can be called webisodes. They can be distributed free of charge through platforms such as YouTube or Vimeo, or through a subscription such as Netflix or Crackle.

Being a new emergent means, the defined definition covers all production made to be distributed for the first time on the Internet, in such a way that duration, theme and genre are indifferent, being able to be of real image or animation.

The standard format of the web series, seasons with episodes of 5 to 15 minutes, has been delivered to the creativity and resources of its producers, so that we see series with limited resources but at the same time other awarded as House of Cards, of the Netflix web television, which received nine Primetime Emmy Award nominations in 2013. In relation to the success of the web series House of Cards and Orange Is the New Black, it has been said: "The two star fictions of the Netflix online platform have It became clear that the traditional consumption model of the series, if there was any doubt, has completely changed, not only have they premiered their second full seasons to consume them on demand but also compete in equal conditions (quality, invoice, actors ... .) with the traditional series and, in addition, it is not broadcast by a television channel. "

Videogame

A video game or video game is an electronic game in which one or more people interact, by means of a controller, with a device that displays video images.1 This electronic device, known generically as "platform", can be a computer , an arcade machine, a video game console or a portable device (a mobile phone, for example). Video games are, year by year, one of the main industries of art and entertainment.

The input device used to manipulate a video game is known as a video game controller, or command, and varies depending on the platform. For example, a controller could only consist of a button and a joystick, while another could have a dozen buttons and one or more levers (command). The first computer games used to make use of a keyboard to carry out the interaction, or they required the user to acquire a joystick with at least one button.2 Many modern computer games allow or require the user to use a keyboard and a mouse simultaneously. Among the most typical drivers are the gamepads, joysticks, keyboards, mice and touch screens.

Generally, video games make use of other ways, apart from the image, to provide the player with interactivity and information. The audio is almost universal, using sound reproduction devices, such as speakers and headphones. Another type of feedback is through haptic peripherals that produce vibration or force feedback, sometimes using vibration to simulate force feedback.

Video blog

A video blog or vlog is a gallery of video clips, ordered chronologically, published by one or more authors. The author can authorize other users to add comments or other videos within the same gallery.

On the web it is scanned, it is not read, 1 so the image takes on a special role, and particularly, the video. If we add to this the evolution of the Web traditionally unidirectional and closed to the participatory Web that Tim O'Reilly rated 2.0, we have as a result an environment where users talk directly and where video platforms like YouTube are significant .

Videoblogs can deal with any topic that the author wants, as with blogs, and the ease of distribution means that some popular videoblogs reach hundreds of thousands of subscribers.2 The aesthetics of a vlog is based on the face-to-face of the blog. vlogger with your audience, speaking, either in an interpretive and acted way, or in a sincere and honest way, connecting directly with him; since the public of a videblogger, being based on both cases, is interested in the videos of the same by the fact of being people with similar tastes, and sometimes, they even get to feel identified. These would only be cases in which the vlogger talks about itself or deals with everyday issues that affect most people. In this way we could classify the different types of vloggers in three broad sectors:

There are vloggers that deal with topics of common interest among an immense majority of people, in this way it gets the attention of more people, thus being able to become more original and getting a wide variety within this branch. They are also, therefore, the most widespread in the YouTube platform. These vloggers can make their videos from a script or in an improvised way, according to the capacities or tastes of the videblogger;

Within these last, many of them also make vlogs in which they tell facts that have happened to them, or any anecdote that they have lived; what would be basically tell your own life, which at first glance may seem boring, but is intended for the public that follows this vlogger for other merits, such as other videos that rise or any other influence they may have within the world of Internet;

We could describe the tutorials as vlogs, although their content is more informative-explanatory, where the vlogger shows the procedure by which something must be done, be it the assembly of a tool, or a makeup tutorial;

Video music clip

A video clip is a short film made mainly for its diffusion in video, television and through internet portals, which offers a representation or visual interpretation of a song. According to various authors, it is the most consumed audiovisual format by global youth.

Video clips are usually made with a multitude of visual and electronic effects. They are very dynamic productions that aim to draw the attention of the viewer. It is the audiovisual genre in which there is more creativity and experimentation. The professionals who operate in this sector must take into account many technical considerations. The music video (or video clip) consists of fields, planes, camera movements of varying complexity and specific lighting treatments. Jailhouse Rock by Elvis Presley, is considered the first video clip in history. The video clip is structured according to the musical theme it represents, that is, its own belonging to the genre is affirmed through a series of visual elements that must be adhered to.

Educational video

The tutorial or educational video is an audiovisual material with some degree of utility in the teaching and learning process. This generic concept encompasses both the didactic video itself (elaborated with an explicit didactic intentionality) and that video that, despite not having been conceived for educational purposes, may be appropriate for the teaching intervention. Educational technology offers several alternatives to promote an adequate learning environment, such as video, which, with the advances and accessibility of new opto-electronic technologies (CD, DVD) and Internet access, is becoming increasingly popular . An adequate use of video as a resource provides various alternatives in its use that can favor the perceptive and cognitive processes during the learning process.

KEY IDEAS OF THIS CHAPTER

▶The genres are specific to each medium of social communication and we must take into account their characteristics to keep us within the genre we choose to produce.

▶The radio gave birth to many of the genres we know today on television, such as telenovelas, video musical and the interview. While videos and other multimedia enabled the Internet to become a medium on stream; that is, in wireless connection, in real time.

▶ Multimedia finds its maximum expression through the preparation of the mechanical effects that once 3D reality programs are edited depending on the multimedia project.

SUGGESTED ACTIVITIES

Make several tours to local media:
. Choose one of your local media and contact them via telephone.
. Make an appointment for your group of students.
. Interview the staff of the environment and ask them about the equipment, logistics and utility.

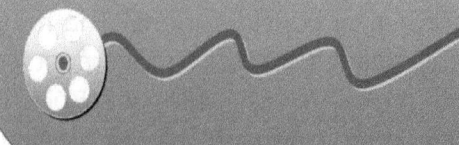

CHAPTER 4

MULTIMEDIA SPACES

- ▶ The Cabin
- ▶ The Studio
- ▶ The location
- ▶ The Digital station

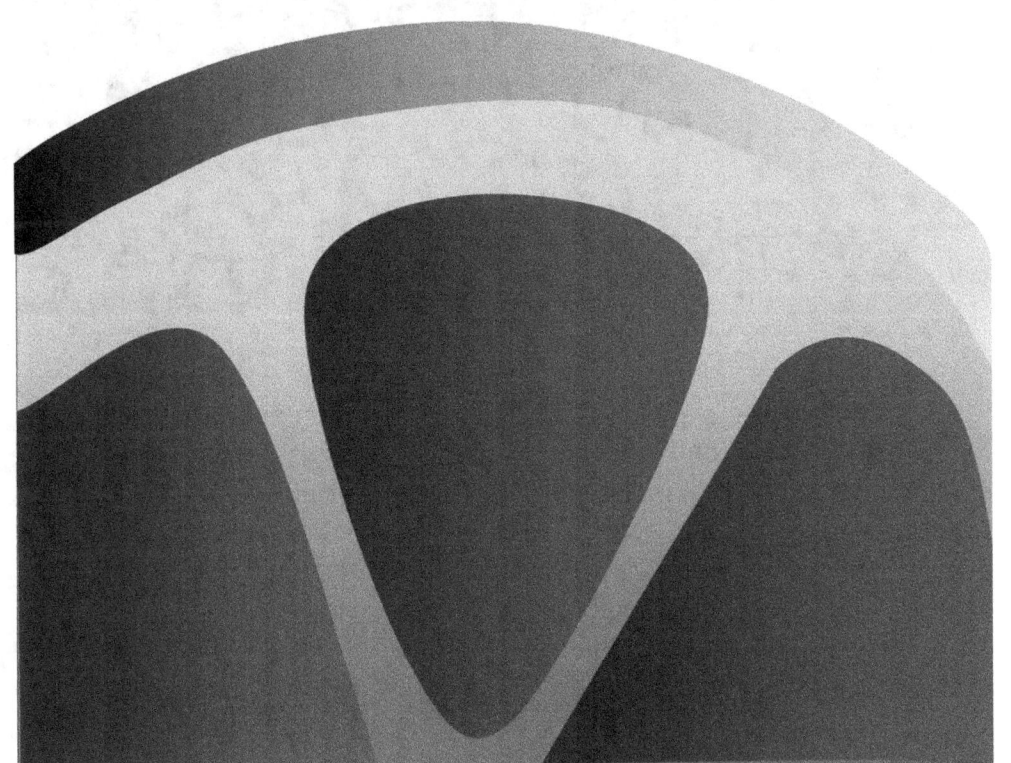

Multimedia Spaces

A place where a film shooting with special effects takes place is not the same as a news studio. For that reason we must learn to distinguish the tools that are at our disposal to achieve each task at the highest professional level, without errors that can be avoided. That is why in this chapter of this book we approach the physical characteristics of each space of four of the main communication media. We compared some differences overcome as well as similar equipment has been replaced by the digital age.

Depending on the location, for the multimedia technician the recording protocol consists of a series of stages: as a selection of equipment available in the warehouse, verification of the wiring, installation of lights and filters in the ceiling, verification of the storage devices, tests of audio and record before the camera, ect.

Then we will study each one with more details.

The Radio Cabin

In a radio station there are several departments such as administration, advertising, the production booth, and the transmission antenna. The special equipment of a cabin have the following characteristics:

• Acoustic insulation in walls, floors, soffits, windows and doors.

• Digital and analog audio recording equipment (computer with audio capture card and audio recording and editing programs)

• An audio mixer with inputs and outputs for canon, rca and 6.1 mm connectors, with 8 channels minimum.

• Four unidirectional and dynamic professional microphones.

• Ergonomic furniture.

• Speakers and audio amplifier.

• Headphones.

• Visual communication between the production booth and speech.

• Air-conditioned environment

• Microphone: Dynamic microphones include ribbon and moving-coil microphones. The first ones have a thin metallic tape attached to the diaphragm, placed in the bosom of a magnetic field. When the sound wave hits the diaphragm and vibrates the tape, a small voltage is generated by electromagnetic induction. The operation of the moving-coil microphone is based on the same principle, but it has a coil of fine wire instead of a ribbon. Some modern microphones, designed to capture only unidirectional sounds, carry a combination of tape and coil. Another type is the condenser microphone. It has two thin metal sheets very close, which act as a condenser. The back sheet is fixed, while the previous one acts as a diaphragm. The sound waves modify the distance between the sheets, altering the electrical capacitance between them. If a microphone of this type is integrated into the corresponding circuit, the variations can be amplified and produce an electrical signal. This type of microphones are usually very small. In the hearing aids, another very common type is used, the electret condenser microphone.

The most important characteristics of any microphone are its response in frequency, directionality, sensitivity and immunity to external disturbances such as shocks or vibrations.

• Sound card: Sound card, expansion card on a computer or computer that allows you to record sounds from a microphone or other external source such as a synthesizer, play them using a speaker or an external amplifier, and sometimes manipulate the sound files stored on the disk. The sound card must have a digital analog converter (CAD), which transforms the incoming sound, analog in nature, into digits that can be stored and processed by the computer. In addition, you must have an analog digital converter (CDA), which converts the stored digital sounds back into an analog wave, which is sent to the speakers.

The AM / FM tuner allows you to listen to programs of radio stations with frequencies between 500 and 1650 kHz for medium wave and between 88 and 108 MHz for FM. From among all the radio signals that reach the antenna, the tuner selects the frequency of the desired station. Next, it extracts the wave from the frequency used to modulate the carrier, thus obtaining the audio signal of the program being transmitted, and amplifies it to activate the loudspeakers of the hi-fi system.

In the normal mechanical-electronic sound recording system, the sound waves are inevitably distorted and pick up noise from the recording process itself. In digital recording these problems do not exist. The digital recorder measures the waves thousands of times per second and assigns a numerical value or digit to each of these measurements. These digits become a stream of electronic pulses that are stored in a memory for subsequent conversion and reproduction. In recent years these techniques have been used in a limited way for the production of conventional gramophone recordings. Currently, direct digital recordings are made, in which the electronic pulses are placed on a compact disc (CD), in which, observed through a microscope, they resemble a signal spiral in Morse code. The CD, once removed from its plastic case, is placed in a computer where a laser beam reads the encoded information and a series of circuits convert it into analog signals for playback through conventional speaker systems.

The amplifier raises the power of the electrical impulses sent by the cartridge until it reaches a sufficient level to activate the speakers. The power that an amplifier can produce is measured in watts (W). Depending on the speaker system, the amplifier can send 10 to 125 W of power or more. In general, the amplifier is controlled by a device called a preamplifier, which amplifies the voltage of the sound signals that are too weak for the amplifier to handle. The preamplifiers also increase the low frequencies and attenuate the high frequencies to compensate for the too weak response of the first and too strong of the second ones in the gramophone recordings. Modern amplifiers are equipped with solid state or integrated circuits.

Speakers or speakers (electromechanical devices that produce audible sound from amplified audio voltages) are widely used in radio receivers, sound systems for films, public services and apparatus to produce sound from a recording, a communication system or a low intensity sound source.

• Speakers: There are different types, but most of the current ones are dynamic. These speakers include a very light wire coil mounted within the magnetic field of a powerful permanent magnet or an electromagnet. A variable electric current from the amplifier passes through the coil and modifies the magnetic force between it and the magnetic field of the speaker. The coil vibrates with current changes and causes a diaphragm or a large vibrating cone, mechanically linked to it, to generate sound waves in the air.

The power and sound quality can be increased by using special sets of several speakers of different sizes (small for high notes and large for serious notes.) The control unit can be considered as the neuralgic center of the hi-fi system, since It performs a series of critical functions, for example, it attenuates the surface noises of old recordings by means of a device called background noise filter and eliminates low frequency noise, such as phonograph motor vibrations. The inability of the human ear to hear the high and low notes with the same clarity with which it listens to the mid frequencies, producing an increase in the relative level of the high and low frequencies when the disc is played at low volume. The control unit also adjusts the sound signals of the turntable, the tape recorder or the tuner.

The Studio

A television studio is the whole complex necessary to put a program on the air. Do not confuse with "set" which is the physical space where what the viewer sees takes place. he television studio is a closed and isolated place of lights, sounds and external magnetic fields, in which you can place audiovisual equipment such as television cameras, professional lighting bulbs, professional sound for recording or retransmission of programs with the highest cleanliness of light, image and sound in the possible environment and necessary to give the broadcast quality necessary to broadcast television programs.

PRODUCTION:

A production is the act through which wealth is created, this activity transforms certain goods into a greater profit, the production team is in charge of the entire organization, and the magnitude of the program and the type of production depends on the producer, who is the responsible for the artistic, creative inputs of the program, the interpretation of the same, the hiring of actors, presenters, supervision of all operations in the study, the producer is the main figure that gives unit cohesion and guidance to the study team. Directs a team specialized in all branches of communication, from stage designers to sound engineer, etc., who also contribute their interpretations of various situations observed in the planning and during the production of the program.

Applied to computers or computers, video recording is synonymous with capturing images from an analog source (for example a video recorder or a video camera) using a dedicated device, capable of converting analog signals to digital format for storage and subsequent treatment with dedicated applications. These devices can be installed on computers in a free PCI slot, by the USB connector or by FireWire connection.

The FireWire connection, called iLink by Sony and other manufacturers, in combination with a video camera or DV video recorder has the advantage over other video capture systems that the quality of the images in their maximum format is preserved at all times (PAL). In general, other non-professional video capture systems use compression systems that partially reduce their quality or perform video capture at a speed of less than 25 frames per second and with a frame size not exceeding 640 × 480 pixels.

The available video applications allow editing, editing, creation and application of special effects, titling and many other tasks on a personal computer and then transfer the finalized project back to analogue support (for playback on a television, by example) or save them to disk with an optimal format for playback from CD-ROM, DVD or Internet support.

The location

In cinematography, the term location (in English, is, in this context, location), when it is related to audiovisual production, refers to a site used in film, television and advertising filming, but which does not It was created with that objective. On-location filming is the practice of filming in a real frame rather than in a sound zone or later area.

In the cinema, a location is any place where a film crew will be filming actors and recording their dialogue. A location where no dialogue is recorded can be considered as a second photo unit site. Filmmakers often choose to shoot on location because they believe that greater realism can be achieved in a "real" place, however outdoor shooting is also often motivated by the movie's budget. For example, the independent horror film Marianne was filmed entirely in Sweden. However, many films record interior scenes in a sound studio and exterior scenes in a location.

It is often mistakenly believed that filming "on location" takes place at the actual location where your story is set, but this is not necessarily the case.

Most movies do a bit of both types of recording, although low-budget films usually do more location shots for higher-budget films, because the cost of filming an existing site is much cheaper than the cost of filming. creation of that place from scratch. In certain situations, it is cheaper to record in a studio. In these situations, low-budget films often record more in a studio.

Recording on location has several advantages of filming in a studio:

• It can be cheaper than building large sets

• The illusion of reality can be stronger - it is hard to replicate real-world-and-tear wear, and architectural details.

• Sometimes it allows the use of cheaper non-union labor or to avoid unemployment in the US.

Its disadvantages include:

Lack of control over the environment - lighting, passing aircraft, traffic, pedestrians, bad weather, city regulations, etc.

Location of a place in the real world that exactly matches the requirements of the script.

Members of the audience may be familiar with a place in the real world used to double as a place of fiction (such as Rumble in the Bronx inexplicably showing the mountains outside Vancouver, at the bottom of an urban scene)

The location can provide a significant benefit in economic development in an area by using equipment from local services, such as catering and lodging.

The digital station

An island is a dark room, with table chairs and digital editing equipment. For the best reception of audio and conversions between storage devices, we usually find an island that is completely HD high definition, which is not completely analogous or is destined to a specific video format, as it is now with AVCHD.

The equipment of a lab or island of editing: In this type of edition you only need a VTR (Video tape recorder) and a computer, which is where the images are going to work.

Computer: We need a CPU with several hard disks of capacity from 1 Tera byte to 4 TB. Previously they were of medium size or if possible large, since the elements that carry inside will have to be well ventilated, so that the storage units do not overheat.

In the computer we will have a MOTHER that is where the platelets or plates are inserted. There we are going to need a DIGITIZER board, which is the one that allows transforming the information from the cassette to digital information that the computer uses.

The images are going to go to a hard disk, but not a conventional one. The hard drive that we need has to be very large (with a lot of data entry capacity, since the images occupy a lot of space on the disk) and with a very high data transfer speed. This is why SCSI-type hard drives (scans) are needed, which have very high data transfer rates. If this type of disc was not used, the images would be cut off. To control this hard disk you need a controller board.

Image quality: With the computer we will be able to choose what image quality we want. The more quality we want, the more it will occupy on the disk, since more information is needed to store. The qualities that we can choose are the following:

Monitors larger than the common ones are used (17 "approx.) Since this way you can gain more space, this is because the windows are shrinking and then we have free space.In order for the windows to shrink, the resolution must be increased.

Timeline: Recording time over the line. There is a line that is divided into seconds. This graduated line can be increased until you can see the pictures.

Editing programs: There are also two horizontal bars parallel to the timeline ("A" and "B") that would be the same as player 1 and 2 on a linear island. Among these, there is another bar called FX (in the Media 100) or T (in the Premiere) of "transition". Below these three bars there are two more audio, called Aa (Audio "a") and Ab (Audio "b").

Bin or Project: This is another window that opens under the TIMELINE, where all the images that we have saved or that we have chosen appear.
• To make an edit: Drag the image that we chose from the BIN, to the A or B of the timeline.
• To make an effect in the transition of images you have to put in the FX or T bar the effect that we choose.

KEY IDEAS OF THIS CHAPTER

▶The television studio and the radio booth are similar in some equipment and in others not so, that is why it is
It is necessary that we know what types of input devices are used in multimedia.

▶The location is a real physical space that gives the cinema the realism that characterizes it. We could never shoot a
indoor movie scene if it were only to control background effects like the chroma key or a snowstorm, or a flood inside a pool, for example.

1. ▶ Multimedia finds its maximum expression through the preparation of the mechanical effects that once 3D reality programs are edited depending on the multimedia project.

SUGGESTED ACTIVITIES

Make several tours to local media:
Choose one of the means and contact them via telephone.
Make an appointment for your group of students.
Interview the staff of the environment and ask them about the equipment, logistics and utility.

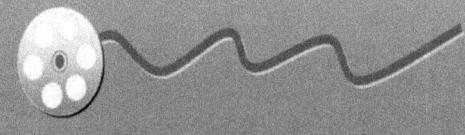

CHAPTER 5

PROJECT DEVELOPMENT

- ▶ The idea
- ▶ Short Bio
- ▶ Adaptations
- ▶ Legal management
- ▶ The 6 questions
- ▶ Types of Contracts
- ▶ Synopsis
- ▶ The Screenwriter and the producer
- ▶ Character Building
- ▶ Treatment or Argument
- ▶ List of Scenes
- ▶ Dialogged continuity
- ▶ The Preliminary Screenplay
- ▶ Script revisions
- ▶ Script format ▶ Script software

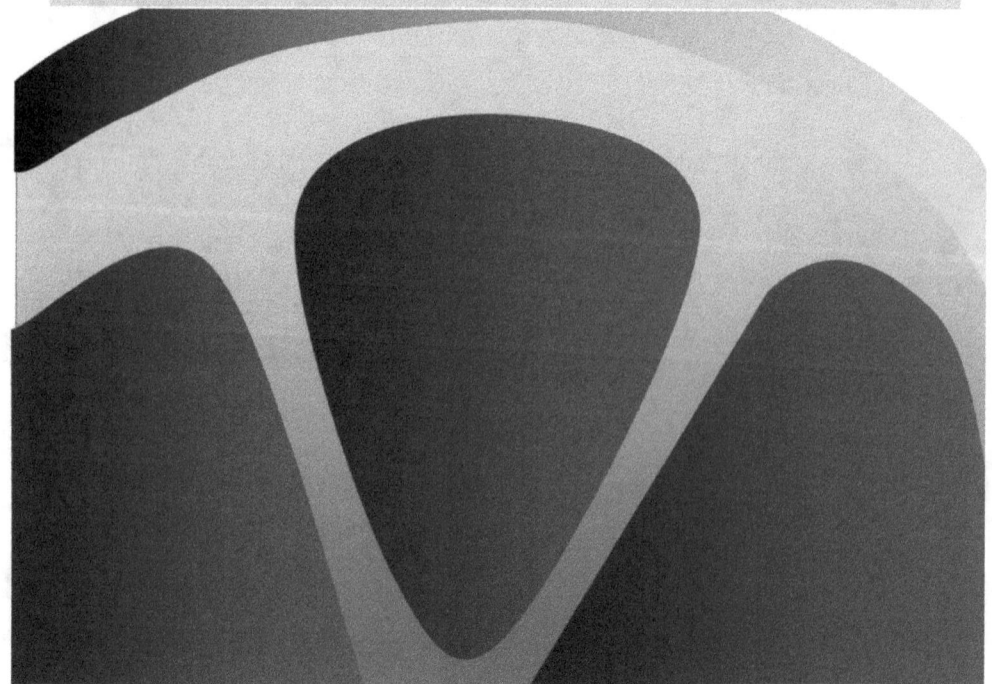

PROJECT DEVELOPMENT

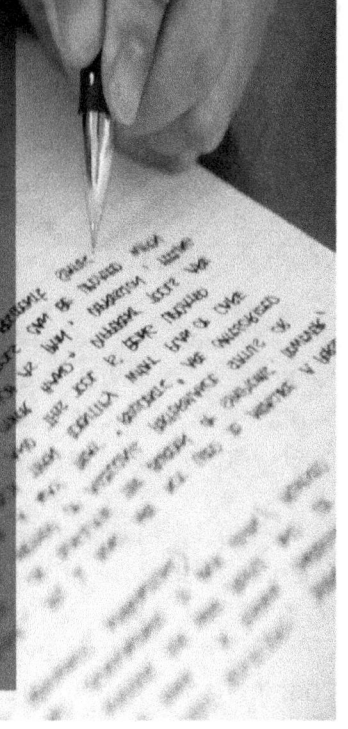

Where to start? If you have a great idea for your multimedia, film, television or any other project media, by following some simple steps you can begin to shape, improve it and sell it to a financial background. You must put a lot of effort into what you propose and not give up by taking your project to happy term. Many ideas seem at first absurd, but with the opportune support they have come to be blockbusters, bookstore hits and the small screen. Writing, drawing, editing and rewriting are just your beginning.

If you already have an idea for a great movie, and do not know where to start or even how a movie script should be, relax your beam just completed one of the most difficult steps is to have an idea.

The art of creative writing of a script can be learned, but all this starts with having a good idea, which are worth gold for the audiovisual industry.

The idea

A good idea can change the world, or at least, guarantee survival, the bread of every day. Ideas are worth money, and since we are people who live by their ideas, nothing is more fair than we charge for them. Of course there are times when we give an idea without charging for it: but in that case it is a gift. Do not despise an idea, even when it seems completely outdated. Always or almost always, it can be used. A good idea can come up on the stamp of a letter, as in the case of Stanley Donen's "Charade" movie, or a simple postcard, as was the case of TB Clarke, who imagined a story from a postcard you received from a friend.

Ideas are worth their own weight, money and therefore must be taken care of. When we have an idea, a script, a title, a play, a lyrics for a song, etc., we must register it immediately. There are organizations that deal with these issues, such as the Authorship Registry of each country.

Just to illustrate, there is the case of Orson Welles. In a talk with Chaplin, Welles mentioned the idea he had for a movie. Days later, Welles travels to Europe. When it returns, isorpresa! The movie Mr. Verdum, written and directed by Chaplin, was already on the eve of being shown. Chaplin had stolen his idea. Welles demanded Chaplin to pay for the use of the idea and credits in the film. Chaplin did not discuss the payment. As we see, some ideas are worth gold.

When we write the story, you can change course and you can even end up in a totally different way. In fact, a synopsis or "story-line" serves as a basis, starting point: there is no rigidity in its development. Now we would like to specify what a "story-line" is not:

- A "" story-line "is not just a statement about life.
- A "story-line" is not just an interrogation about life.
- A "story-line" is not only the moral of the story.

Let's go to another example of what a "story-line" is through Graham Greene, the famous English screenwriter.

Idea: "I went to the funeral of a friend. Three days later, he was walking the streets of New York. "

From there came the next "story-line" that gave rise to the film "The Third Man".

Story-line: "Jack goes to his friend's funeral in Vienna. Without resigning himself to this loss, he investigates and ends up discovering that his friend did not die. He is alive and forged his funeral because he was being wanted by the police. Discovered by Jack's curiosity, the friend ends up shot dead by the police. "

Do not try more explanations or instead of a "story-line" we will have a treatment or argument.

These exercises were applied in the course of scripts in Rio de Janeiro, 1982 Arts Center of Laranjeiras. We decided to include them in the book so that the reader has an idea of how to exercise and so that he can see how an idea evolves, from the simple idea to the Argument. We can also observe how, the same idea is used by different people.

A possible first exercise would be the following. The students were asked to write 5 ideas. Of all these ideas, the group of students chose 2 to be developed.

1. A ladder that grows.

2. A woman goes crazy and starts to drag the iron as if it were a dog.

1° Synopsis on the topic Escalera: "Knowing that a man has visions and believes that the staircase of an abandoned house moves in several directions, a group of merchants, with the intention of making their business progress, spread the word of that Our Lady appears at the top of the stairs. People from all places come to the place: not only the merchants but the whole city progresses quickly. "

Observations: Incomplete. The solution to the conflict and more details about man and his visions fail.

Questions: Does the ladder really move? What is the drama of this name?

2 °) Synopsis of the idea of the Iron: "In a country occupied by the Nazis, a woman who carries an iron and a thousand pranks is called by all as the crazy folk of the city. In reality, she is the link between different foci of the armed resistance, and it carries within the grid fundamental messages for the organization of the movement. The invaders never think about revising it. After the final victory of the police, the madwoman of the iron becomes a nation heroine. "

Observation: Completo. There is development, conflict and solution.

Now let's see a comedy-satirical cross.

"Solitary and despised by their respective families, an old man and an old woman open a brothel, thus calling the attention of their relatives causing a major scandal in the town."

If we modify it, it would be like this: "A couple of old people discover that they have little money left Resigned, resolve to dedicate themselves to love They open a brothel only for the elderly They have great success and are rejected by society They both die of an orgasm."

Your idea probably comes from one of these resources:
1. This is an original idea that you thought on the way to work, in the car, or in the morning in the bathroom.
2. This idea is from a book you read and you think it can become a great movie.
3. It is from a magazine or newspaper article and becomes the basis of your script.

4. It's the life story of someone famous or somehow inspired you.

TYPES OF IDEAS:

Transformed idea

A Transformed Idea is basically an idea that is inspired by a fiction, a movie, a book, a play that we saw but we would like to tell in our own way by giving it several personal turns. Among us, scriptwriters, we say that "the amateur author copies from his successful colleagues, while the professional author steals ... and transforms". Enrique V, of the illustrious English author Shakespeare, was an idea stolen from a work written by another author of the time. However, it is necessary to point out the difference between a Plagiarism and a Transformed Idea. Plagiarism is the transcription "ipsis literis" of parts of a work, while Idea Transformed is to use the same idea in another way.

Idea requested

Idea Requested is the idea made on request. A producer asks us for a script about the story inspired by what happens in a certain location, or for an educational film and from there, we think about the subject.

Research idea

An Investigated Idea is one in which we use research to find out what kind of film is missing in the market. An investigation can show that in Brazil there is no period film. For example about conflicts between Portuguese and Indians. The Investigated Idea is one that occupies a void in the market. Another type of Investigated Idea is when a film, (show, play, etc.) is directed to a specific audience; that's common on television.

The film Apocalypse Now, by Francis Copola, was made on a subject that had not yet been taken into account in the war films: Vietnam. Finally, the idea investigated is the idea that responds to a thematic gap, both dramatic and commercial. The classic example of an investigated idea that did not work was the movie Cleopatra. Commercially it had everything to be a success: a well-known story, Elizabeth Taylor, Richard Burton and a lot of luxury. Happy or unhappily, the public did not like the idea.

Short Bio

Exercise No.1

Fill this idea sheet to devise a character can be someone you love, someone you do not love so much, a friend, a platonic love, a celebrity, a neighbor ... whatever you can think of. Then, based on this information, create the synopsis of your opera prima.

IDEA SHEET

1. GENERAL

Temporality (dates)
Preliminary title:
Protagonist or central character:
Dominant need of the protagonist:
Dramatic premise:
Other important characters:
Place:
Chance:
Conflict or main dilemma:
How your character changes at the end:
Resolution:

2. SHORT BIOGRAPHY

Name of the protagonist:
Physical characteristics:
o Age:
o Day of birth:
o Skin Color:
o Eye color:
o Hair color:
o Posture:
o Appearance:
o Voice tone:
o General appearance:

3. FAMILY SITUATION:

o Nature of the relationship:
o Father:
o Mom:
o Relatives:
o Other important relatives:
o Family functionality:
o Marital status:
o Children:
o Sex life:
or Intimate friends:

4. PLACE IN THE COMMUNITY:

o Occupation:
o Education:
o Economic class:
or political affiliation:
or religious affiliation:
o Membership in other institutions:
o General status in the community:

o Leisure activities:

5. INTERNAL WORLD:

or Intelligence:
o Personality type:
o Sense of self-confidence:
o Degree of sexual satisfaction:
o Sense of morality:
o Important secrets:

o Personal goals:
o Important setbacks:
o Special qualities and talents:

Adaptations

When making a script for the first time, it may be easier for you to adapt a literary work than to completely invent the story. A novel will almost always be too long, but it is easy to condense a story of reasonable length. Do not change the argument too much, and avoid altering the dialogues as much as possible.

If you have already found a story that fits your intentions, and you intend to send the film to a contest or to any form of public exhibition, you must consider the copyright issue. If the work is more than fifty years old, there is no problem, but if it is more recent you must obtain the permission of the author or lawyer of the right-holder. Apart from this, each production includes its own copyright, even if the original was more than fifty years old. If the film is going to be shown locally or internationally. Obtaining the permit will not be difficult and may also require little money. In general, publishers worry about claiming their rights only if they consider that money is made with the film.

The beginning scriptwriter, generally believes that it is easier to adapt than to write an original. To imagine that an adaptation is easier than an original is a monumental error. An adaptation is a transcription of the language in which we change the linguistic support used to tell a story. This is equivalent to the act of transubstantiation, that is to transform the substance, since a work is the expression of language.

Therefore, since a work is a unit of content and form, at the moment in which we appropriate ourselves when we only appropriate the content and we express it through another language, we necessarily enter into the process of recreation.

Of course, this act of recreating implies the risk that the recreated product is below the original. However sometimes it happens that the adaptation exceeds the original.

That happens because sometimes the material of the story lends itself better to another type of dramatic support. An adaptation involves the choice of a work adaptable, that is, that can be transported without loss of quality. Not all works lend themselves to transcription. A typical example of impossibility of transcription is the novel Ulysses, by James Joyce, given that what characterizes this novel is the flow of consciousness; mental facts within the character.

An adaptation implies a creative limit since the scriptwriter must adhere to the content of the work, that is to say to its climates, characters, intentions, etc. But as we saw, that limit can be positive and from it a better original work can be born. Of course, this depends on the talent of the screenwriter. Millor Fernández says that his translation of Moliere improves the original because with his knowledge and his technique. Millor adds other qualities to Moliere. We must think like Millor when making an adaptation.

Theater

The great advantage of adapting a play comes from the fact that the main dialogues are ready and that the material was already created based on the living word, presupposing the body-to-body relationship and that of audience and actor.

One difficulty in adapting a theatrical work is that the stage is limiting, while the camera has amplitude. Another reason is that the dialogues relate what is happening offstage instead of showing the scenes. That means that the work has to be unfolded and increased, breaking the existing dramatic rhythm. Everything that is spoken in a play, in the film version, must be shown with sequences of shots.

When a work is vintage and the writer wants to transport it to another time and place, it is not an adaptation, but a recreation. An adaptation presupposes that the story is maintained in its entirety, respecting the number of characters, places, epochs, etc. In the case of a recreation, the scriptwriter must indicate that the script is "Based on the work of ..." Being that way, adapting means transporting from one medium or channel of communication to another, a message of its own, adapting the content of the original work to another support.

The Story

Given the basic characteristic of the story: the synthesis, the brevity of a story may contain enough material for a whole series. Therefore, in the work of adapting a story, we find the material in its most condensed form and from there we will build everything: the dialogue, the dramatic action, the characters, parallel "plots", etc. In all this we must maintain the spirit of the work. Although the scriptwriter is free to add or modify some aspects of the work, the basic characteristics must be maintained. The work has to be recognizable. That care is important: we can recreate, add but never de-characterize or deface the original work.

The novel

In the novel, contrary to what happens in the story or in the play, the adaptation work focuses on the condensation of the work, eliminating the facts that are not essential or viable for funding, emphasizing the main dramatic core of the work, the backbone of the novel. Rarely a novel has dialogues: then the scriptwriter must create the dialogues, based on the profile of the characters, respecting to the maximum the indications of the original author of the argument used for our adapted script.

The adaptable material has different forms, but the first question we must ask ourselves is whether the work is really adaptable. Contrary to what Nyemeyer says ("any stroke in pencil can be translated in concrete") not all works made to be read can be seen. Buñuel tried 3 adaptations of the novel "Under the volcano". Malcolm Lorry: none of them served. Then, when a scriptwriter wishes to adapt a work, he must pay attention to the following factors:

- If the work is translatable into a cinematographic or television language.

- You must follow the same process of creating an original, that is, make a "story-line", develop an argument. etc.

- Reduce the pretext until obtaining the main elements and start working.

- Have time for reflection.

- To be faithful to the original, while avoiding simple transport, it is essential to transform without transfiguring.

- Be attentive to the questions of Right of Authorship.

These data are basically the main ones in any adaptation work. The rest depends exclusively on the talent of the script adapter.

A proper narration

When looking for a story to adapt to the cinema, always think about its adaptation to the new media. Thus, it is easy to imagine ideas such as remorse or lack of money while reading, but it is not so easy to pass them to the cinema. Thoughts and inner conflicts must be illustrated on the screen, but you must be able to translate them accurately into the language of the image and sound. Therefore, an amateur should seek a narrative with a clear argument, few characters, plausible dialogue and without too much "psychological" action.

Once you choose, you have to think about the turn that you want to give, which is a summary of the screenwriter's vision of the film. If it will be used for an animated film or the film will require special effects, from it the storyboard is drawn and with it the technical script. Once the scenarios have been located, the filming plan. The scenarios should be chosen as carefully as the story, because they will determine to a large extent the particular atmosphere of the film; they have to enjoy a suitable light, to be able to roll free of voyeurs, undesirable sounds of cars, bad weather, airplanes and other undesirable interruptions.

The original narration

The Henry James narrative "Years of maturity" will serve well as an example of cinematographic visualization of the inner life. It tells the story of a sick, but still inspired, convalescent writer in Bournemouth, a seaside resort in England. Here he receives a copy of the last novel he will write in his life. The opening scene proceeds as follows.

"It was a peaceful and luminous April day, and poor Dencombe, happy in the presumption of the recovered forces, walked through the hotel garden appreciating, with the dilatoriness of those who are still convalescing, the attractions of a quiet walk. He liked to feel the south as someone from the north feels, he liked the shady cliffs and the pines crowded, he liked even the faded sea. "Bournemouth sanatorium" now seemed like a simple advertisement, but he was grateful with all his soul for the most ordinary comforts. The talkative rural mailman had just entered the garden to deliver a *small package that he took with him, leaving the hotel on the right and walking painfully to a bench he used to frequent, a safe refuge by the cliff. He looked south, toward the woven escarpments of the island, and the gentle slope of the hill protected him from behind. When he arrived he was really tired and, for a moment, even disappointed; he felt better, that of course, but better than what? Could he ever return to this: -as he was in one or two key moments of his past- better than himself?*

Dencombe looked towards the sea, observed a group of people and opened the package ... "

Locate the exteriors taking into account the narration. Write down the hours when the light is adequate and ask the potential owners of the land for the permission necessary for the time when it is going to roll. If you want on the street with a tripod, you should inform yourself beforehand.

STAGES OF THE SCRIPT

Usually and before arriving at the script itself, the preparation of a film contains several stages. (As introduced by Zavattini, 1953).

• The argument.

• The treatment.

• The pre-script

• The script.

1. The argument. His text has the appearance of a short story and also its form is literary. There is no technical or ambience indication in it.

2. The treatment. In this second text the narrative notes of the argument are developed and expanded. The form is still literary, but it has already acquired more defined narrative characteristics based on the description

of the different scenes in which the plot is divided, paying particular attention to the setting (even the city and the place where they are needed are specified). the action takes place) and the concretion of the situations.

3. The pre-script. In this phase, the project is presented as a description of all the scenes, with summary indications of what happens in each one of them.

4. The script. Finally, the schematic pre-script indications are fully developed in the script.

- The reproduced fragments already have the form of the literary script, but they lack the technical indications referred to the subdivision in planes, to the type of framing, etc., own indications of what, in the cinematographic jargon is denominated technical script. This is something that the director and his closest collaborators are in charge of elaborating in different ways.

- Thus it can be said that the final script allows, sometimes, a certain degree of improvisation both in the set itself and in the editing room, when variations in the material can still be introduced.

Synopsis

All screenwriters use synopsis to sell their scripts. In Latin America, the opportunities to achieve this are limited to international competitions announced on the Internet and, for those who wish to go further, it is also the case of contacts made in co-production forums held in other countries.

We use synopsis along with letters of intent to impress jurors and agents that we have never met. This is how we present to project competitions to encourage judges to read our scripts. We communicate already registered, to attract producers who live thousands of miles from us. We have a lot of synopses, and we need the synopsis that makes the difference.

The first step towards the sale of a script:

In some situations, the synopsis works better as a sales tool as a script does. Agents and producers seek the simple way to negotiate are nonproduced screenwriters. The synopses provide less for them to say no than a detailed argument or a finished script does. This can be an advantage.

As they become familiar with the our film idea, they exercise their own imagination. This will take them one step further to ask to read the script.

CREATING A DYNAMIC SYNOPSIS

The techniques for creating a short synopsis vary among screenwriters but most will agree with the warning that says, "If you can not say it in three sentences, you're not sure what your script will be about."

Some writers simply summarize their films: presentation, conflict and resolution. Other writers create a prayer in the style of television guides emphasizing both sides of the drama, both internally and externally. An example can be the synopsis of the film of E.T .:

"A shy, alienated boy contacts a young alien who was left on Earth; the boy convinces the adults to help the alien by contacting his mother ship so he can return to his planet. "

A wise suggestion is not to limit yourself to establishing an argument, to emphasize the unique elements of your script allow the audience to connect with the situation and build with the hero. Think of your synopsis as a vivid trailer for your movie. Here we will show you what we want to say to create synopsis of two popular movies:

• Synopsis for "Character" movie: Rain Man

"A young man, self-centered and brave, returns home for his father's funeral and realizes that he has been disinherited. The wealth of the family is left to an older autistic brother that he never knew he had. "

To create "identification" with the protagonist we have to show moments that emphasize the contrast between brothers and dramatize the frustration of this unexpected obstacle in their ambitions.

To create "connection" with the situation of the protagonists we have to show the actions they take to get what they want, the family inheritance. How they try to control the inheritance. He kidnaps his autistic brother. Since their autistic brother is afraid to take the flight, they drive through the country. They visit Las Vegas, shopping centers where the ambitious brother feels good but the autistic brother thanks and produces pity.

The climax of the "potential crisis" of the protagonist is to face the moment in which the relationship with his brother has learned what happened.

To emphasize the "risk" of the ambitious brother, we put a threat and unveil the great secret of the brother.

Finally, adding these key points, we will obtain a synopsis of more than 5 lines that will allow us to expand it to the next step, which is the treatment in 5 to 12 pages.

REVISED SYNOPSIS OF "RAIN MAN"

"An ambitious and self-centered man returns home for his father's funeral and learns that his inheritance has been left to an autistic brother he did not know. The ambitious kidnaps his autistic brother and drives across the country hoping to gain his trust and thus gain control of the family's money. The trip reveals the unusual dimension of his brother's autism and unravels a childhood secret that will change everything. "

This synopsis could convince you to read the script. Let's see another example.

• Movie synopsis based on his "Argument": SOME LIKE IT HOT

"Two musicians are witnesses of the Day of the Saint Valentine Massacre. When the thugs chase them, they try to elude them by joining a gang of girls on a Miami yacht. "

What movie would we like to use to create a trailer for this classic comedy? What we want to emphasize is the acceleration of the "comic" complications that are the result of the intersection of the comedy-action genres. Let's now think about the objectives of each one:

»The saxophonist is so in love with a sexy girl from the band that he creates a new identity to persuade her.

»The bassist struggles to stay jovial as well as uses tricks to hide his age, close to the one his seductive partner customizes.

If we want to reveal the "dangerous" implications that the massacred crowd promises to face. We must reveal that the thugs show up at the Miami resort where the girls have their yacht to complicate the love and put pressure on the heroes. "

"Two musicians are witnesses of the Day of the Saint Valentine Massacre. When the thugs chase them, they try to elude them by joining a gang of girls on a Miami yacht. The saxophonist is so in love with a sexy girl from the band that creates a new identity to persuade her. The bassist struggles to stay jovial as well as uses tricks to hide his age, close to the one his seductive partner customizes. Love conquers everything until the thugs arrive during a convention at the Miami resort. "

We would like to read this script.

Answer these questions to review your synopsis:

- Does your synopsis reveal the situation of your protagonist?
- Does your synopsis reveal the most important implications?
- Describe the actions taken by your protagonist?
- Describe your crisis?
- Does it show the climax (the danger and its culmination)?
- Does the protagonist show a potential transformation?
- Is it hot: shows sex, greed, humor, danger, suspense and satisfaction?
- Is it identified?
- Is the synopsis between three sentences in the present tense maintained?

How can you pack your idea in three sentences? If you think that your synopsis looks like the commercial of a movie that you have seen in your head, as well as you have been writing the script, you will give life to those three sentences.

Character Building

This does not mean that all the characters should be nice or nice or admirable, Don Corleone in "The Godfather" and Sidney Falco in "The Sweet Smell of Success" are neither admirable nor pleasant but antiheroes; however, you can tell an exciting story about them. A despicable character, but with a slight chance of salvation, can be as easily a protagonist as a fun and admirable character. In the same way, a sympathetic character must have its undesirable side if you want to create tension in the audience about whether he or she will be able to do what they have to do to reach their goal.

It should be noted that our interest in whether the protagonist reaches his goal is proportional to the interest of that character to reach his goal. The more intense your desire, the greater our concern. We do not ask if what the protagonist seeks is moral or immoral, just or unjust, generous or selfish; we ask how strongly the protagonist wants that something and that determines our emotional attitude towards him. A protagonist who does not know what he wants, or knows but does not care much whether he gets it or not, represents a poor dramatic material.

Imagine how worried we would be for a protagonist who decides that the Path he is traveling is very dangerous and hides to let things be solved alone. Or how much we would worry about the repentant gunman who hangs up his revolvers and swears he will not use them again, but at the first sign of trouble, he puts on his guns and reassumes his old behavior.

It is the fight of the character, man or woman, full virtues and defects, which catches the audience and makes you worry about the development of the story.

In the movies, the protagonist almost always has the main role, the most interesting, and is the character that is most on screen, for the simple reason that it is the destiny of that person that we are following. Writers often name their films with the name of the protagonist: Erin Brockovich, Donnie Brasco, Michael Collins, Citizen Kane, Ninotchka, Tootsie - the list is endless. From time to time we find a story where two people want more or less the same thing and struggle to achieve almost the same goal. But in these stories, like "Bonnie and Clyde" and "Butch Cassidy and the Sundance Kid", the protagonist is usually the person who makes the decisions that mega the story develops, change. In these cases, Clyde and Butch, who have no more time on screen than their peers, but are the protagonists because their actions are imitated by the partner, their decisions make history develop and their desires are imposed on those of the partner.

A. OBJECTIVE OF THE CHARACTER:

Only by having a clear vision of the protagonist's objectives is that a film history can be planned, because the search for that objective determines the course of the action, no matter how straight or deviant the path may be. These are the three main points about the protagonist and his goal:

1. There can only be one main objective for the film to have unity. In a story with a protagonist that has more than one goal, the conclusion must be presented, whether success or failure, of each struggle to achieve each goal before moving on to the next, and this is very difficult to structure in a story and It can dispel the interest of the audience.

A script is like a suspension bridge, with one end anchored in what the protagonist wants, and the other end anchored to the outcome if it succeeds or not depends on the author. A bridge that bifurcates in the middle towards two different paths can never be structurally good.

2. The objective must be able to arouse the opposition necessary for conflict to occur. Whether the opposition comes from another person (the "nemesis") of the nature of the circumstances of the story, or the protagonist himself, the story is much stronger if the struggle for an objective finds active opposition, that if he does not find opposition.

3. The nature of the objective is a major factor in determining the attitude of the audience towards the protagonist and the opposition that is found. If the objective is heroic, we will probably admire the protagonist. If the objective is quixotic, we may have fun. A detestable goal will awaken our hatred or discomfort towards the main character, and so on. The protagonist and his goal are so closely identified in our minds to the point that it is impossible to consider one without the other.

B. CONFLICT

The keyword is always conflict. What is the conflict of history? What is the conflict that will mark the story you want to tell?

The conflict is a vital element of each dramatic work, either on stage or in the film. Without conflict history will not catch the audience. A story shows a protagonist struggling to achieve a specific goal, a goal that is difficult to achieve, and whose achievement finds active opposition. Conflict is the element that drives history forward, it is what provides the energy and dynamism of history. Without conflict, a film story could not have life. The need for conflict can not be ignored.

There is a tendency for the beginning scriptwriter to think of conflict as something that involves shouting, guns, fists, or other forms of extreme behavior. While all of these things may contain conflict, they are not the only ways to show it. A character simply trying to eat his lunch can escalate to a conflict enough to give weight to a scene. In a memorable "Five Easy Pieces" scene, Robert Dupea tries to order toast to accompany his meal, what could be a dull moment becomes a fascinating scene when the toast turns into a clash of wills between Dupea and a waitress who It clings to the restaurant's rules of not replacing menu foods.

The conflict is not created by exaggerated actions or excessive behaviors, it is created when a character wants something that is difficult to obtain. This is the same in the whole story or in an individual scene. If no character wants anything in a scene, there is no conflict, and the same scene is poor, without form or effect. If no character wants anything in the whole story, the script falls into the same fault.

Wanting something can be positive or negative. For the purpose, not wanting to do something is as strong as wanting something actively. Trying to get out of a situation or to return to a more desirable life condition is to want something. Trying to do something difficult creates conflict. The desire that creates the conflict can be as simple as trying to put on a pair of boots, as in the opening scene of "Dance with Wolves", or as cataclysmic as saving the world from nuclear destruction, as in "Dr.Strangelove" or in many James Bond movies. Not wanting to do something can be a powerful desire, like Rick in "Casablana" who takes no risks for anyone. Wanting to return home is what moves both the book and the movie "The Wizard of Oz".

C. OBSTACLES

When our characters are alive, we soon understand that we are driving, if not following, and that is when writing and telling stories becomes magic.

If the protagonist and his objective constitute the first two key elements in the construction of a story, the different obstacles constitute the third. Without impediments to achieve the wishes of the protagonist conflict or history. The protagonist would simply achieve his goal without much difficulty. This is very good in real life, but it is fatal to the drama, because without struggle to reach a desired goal you can not keep the attention of the audience.

There may only be one obstacle, and this can be simple and easily identifiable. A murderous humanoid machine of the future is scheduled to kill Sarah in "Terminator"; the people of Vandamm have mistaken Roger Thornhill for a fictional spy named Roger Kaplan in "North by Northwest"; Nurse Ratched is determined to break the spirit of McMurphy in "Someone Volo Over the Cuckoo's Nest". When there is a well-defined opponent character, he or she is known as "the antagonist" (or nemesis and villain).

On the other hand, there may be several obstacles, Jake's struggle to discover the secrets behind the murder in "Chinatown" is hampered by Noah Cross, by the police and even by its main ally, Evelyn Mulwray, who refuses to be honest and tell him the whole truth. Jim's struggle to find himself and his place in the world in "Rebel Without a Cause" not only finds resistance in his parents, but also in school, in the community, and in Jim himself, who has many doubts and a great insecurity.

There may be several obstacles, and they appear one after the other. Romeo and Juliet can not openly declare their love for the enmity of their families, but they also have to face a series of complications: Romeo is exiled for murdering Thybald; Juliet's parents, unaware of her marriage to Romeo, insist that she marry Paris: the message of Father Lawrence; to Romeo informing that Juliet has taken a potion does not arrive; assuming her dead, Romeo tries to reach Juliet's grave, but first she must fight a duel with Paris; Juliet, upon awakening finds that Romeo has committed suicide. Only when Juliet is killed can the two lovers meet again. Richard Blaney, in "Frenzy", is first dismissed from a small-time job; then he makes friends with a man who turns out to be a ruthless serial killer; the murderer kills Blaney's ex-wife, with whom he just had a fight; and the murderer then kills Blaney's girlfriend, who has helped him hide from the police, who thinks Blaney is the killer.

Finally, the obstacles can be very subtle and complex, as in "Sex, lies and videotape" and "Thelma and Louise". The protagonist and the obstacles he finds must be made to their proper measure. If the obstacle is then to reach the goal of history, it has no life. But the obstacle can not be so overwhelming that the protagonist does not have the opportunity to overcome it. In other words, the goal must be possible but very difficult to achieve.

This point can be contradictory in films like "The Third Man" and "Death of a Seller", where a past action puts an overwhelming weight against the achievement of the goal. It is important to know that the protagonists do not recognize that failure is inevitable until the last moment.

Even when they have all the odds against them, they keep fighting and believing that they have an opportunity to succeed; and this belief of the character is what keeps the story alive, and what gives us the necessary dose of hope that the character can achieve his goal.

A distinction must be made between conflict and problems. Punctured tires, lost wallets, and defective answering machines are inconveniences of daily life that can seem formidable conflicts. But in drama these inconveniences could be conflicts or problems. The determining factor is whether the inconvenience is truly an obstacle to fulfill a wish, achieve an objective or achieve a goal. A boyfriend trying to get to church on time has a flat tire and is an obstacle, creating a conflict through a chain of problems. There is something at stake that the flat tire puts in danger. But if there is neither desire nor goal nor goal, if there is nothing at stake for the character, then the flat tire is simply an inconvenience without major consequences. If there is not something at stake for at least one character, a particular event in the story will not have a dramatic impact, no matter how conflictive it may seem on the surface.

One last point, very important: Although the unity of the unity of the story depends on the existence of a single main objective, there is no threat against unity if multiple obstacles are used against the achievement of that objective.

D. PREMISE AND HOME

If the film has a lot of action and emotion at the beginning, somewhere in that beginning there has to be some explanation or development of the character, which will produce a collapse in the story like 20 minutes after starting with a spectacular beginning. A soft start is preferable. The audience will forgive you almost anything at the beginning of the movie, but almost nothing at the end. If you are not satisfied with the end, nothing that has happened before then will help.

The beginning of the story is any arbitrary point, which is selected by the writer in a larger story. The circumstances that have led to the conflict that is presented in the script can usually be attributed to things that happened long before the initial FADE IN. Most of "The Godfather II" is the story of Don Corleone before the events covered in "The Godfather". The first trilogy of "Star Wars" are chapters four, five and six of a series of nine chapters developed by George Lucas.

The premise is a word particularly misused and misinterpreted in the dramatic context. In logic, the premise is part of a syllogism: All humans have blood in their veins (major premise); I am human (minor premise); therefore, I have blood in my veins (conclusion). In drama, "there are parallels close to logic. One way of looking at history is that a protagonist and his goal (major premise) against the antagonist and the obstacles (minor premise) lead to the drama and the emotional response of the audience (conclusion). If a story presents an internal conflict then protagonist and antagonist are two parts of the personality of the central character. In opposite form, if history presents an external conflict, the protagonist and the antagonist are two separate characters. In some cases the antagonist is really the circumstance, as in a man's story against nature.

The premise, as we will use the term in this course, is simply the complex situation that exists when at the beginning of the story the protagonist begins to walk towards his goal. This includes all the reference information pertinent to the story.

The protagonist, his potential desire for the goal, and the potential obstacles (including the antagonist) to reach the goal. You have to know all these elements, so that it appears as the story unfolds.

The beginning, unlike the premise, is that point in the story selected by the writer to start the film.

Following the premises and beginnings of four stories:

1. Rick owns a fashionable nightclub in Casablanca at the beginning of World War II. A man with a past who fought before for lost causes, now Rick has hardened and is not willing to risk his neck for anyone. The screenwriter of "Casablanca" chooses to start the story with quick capsules of the world situation and a demonstration of the dangers in the world. Then we quickly reach the point where Ilsa, the woman in Rick's past, enters Rick's bar.

2. The Capulets and Montagues have been enemies for years. Romeo, a young impulsive and heir of the Montagues, and Juliet, the sensitive daughter of the Capulets, fall deeply in love. Shakespeare chooses to start his work with a street fight that dramatizes the enmity of the two families, then moves quickly to a dance offered by the Capulets, where Romeo arrives as a parachutist and meets Julieta.

3. John Book is a tough and cynical Philadelphia homicide detective who is assigned to investigate the crime of an undercover police officer at a train station. His only witness is a boy, Amish, who travels with his young widowed mother. The screenwriters of "Witness" chose to present us the Amish world of the boy and his mother, and then subtly demonstrate the horrors of city life with crime.

4. Chief Brody is the commissar of a small island community. He used to be a city policeman and, although he fears the sea, he has moved to a quiet town surrounded by water. A great white shark attacks and almost devours a young bather, and seems to remain close to the paradisiacal summer island. For the beginning, the scriptwriters of

"Shark" chose a demonstration of the ferocious and horrifying power of the shark, then they went quickly to land, firm, to establish the world of the main character before the first attack of the shark was known.

Many scripts are conceived in the mind of the writer around situations that are, in essence, premises. A satisfactory premise always contains the potential for conflict and some pertinent and specific information about the main character. Once the way to start the film has been chosen, the beginning of that conflict should not take long.

E. MAIN TENSION, CULMINATION AND RESOLUTION

In the drama, the essential thing is the character change. The character at the end is not the same as at the beginning. He has changed psychologically and even physically.

The audiences do not want to be played with them. They are so interested in seeing true human behavior. They want to be surprised, they want to be entertained. This does not necessarily mean a happy ending, but some kind of closure.

The average script contains several minor climaxes and resolutions, scene after scene and sequence after sequence, but in this section we will concentrate only on the main tension of the second act, its culmination, and the resolution of the main conflict in the story.

Beginning screenwriters often confuse culmination and resolution and think that there is only one climax in a film story. But in fact, in the traditional structure of the three acts, where the second act is about half the story, the main tension is only the conflict of the second act. When the culmination is resolved a new tension is created, which, in its simplest form, can be described as "What will happen?", And this leads directly (with twists and turns) towards the resolution of the whole story.

For example, in "Chinatown," the main tension is not whether "Can Jake help Evelyn and her daughter escape the clutches of Noah Cross?" By the time the main tension is established (at the end of the first act we do not know In that moment, the main tension is "Will Jake be able to discover who and what is behind the deception that made him look ridiculous?" This is what Jake tries to decipher during the second act. by solving that mystery they create most of the movie.When Jake has solved the mystery and knows all about Evelyn, Noah, the daughter, and who murdered Hollis Mulwray, then a new tension is created: "Jake can help Evelyn and Did your daughter escape from Noah's clutches? "That's the tension of the third act and the resolution is that Jake is not capable, Evelyn dies, and Noah stays with his daughter.

Treatment or Argument

The work of the scriptwriter is to reorder the chronology of the narrative so that the flashbacks, memories and concerns of the characters are understandable to the audience. Sometimes it is necessary to add some kind of action to link the scenes, but you should avoid adding dialogue. Example:

"Bournemouth in the late 1890s. A spring day, in the morning. We see the sandy cliffs that are collapsing on the sea, and by which a mailman approaches, whistling. Tie the horse at the entrance of the hotel and enter the garden with the bag. At this moment a man comes out of the hotel and heads on a cane with an uncertain step towards the pines. The mailman calls him and tells him he has a package. Dencombe, that's the man's name, take the package and walk to the right of the hotel, to a bench overlooking the sea. He is at the end of the fifties, very thin and with a clearly precarious health. The effort to reach the bank leaves him almost exhausted. Look carefully and with a hint of humor to a group of three people - a couple of young people and an older woman - who are on the beach, and then dedicate themselves to the package. Read the address (Bournemouth) and the name. He opens it and looks at the title: Years of maturity, of Dencombe himself, which is also the title of the film. He leafs through the book and sighs, while, he says to himself: "Oh, who had another chance, a little bit of luck ..." (The original dialogue.)

It is a treatment of the scene, perhaps a little summarized, but it gives an idea of the technique to be used. The chronology has been reversed, and now the postman is the first to appear. The name, profession and residence of the writer are seen and heard, and their weaknesses become evident.

ARGUMENT OR TREATMENT

The argument or treatment is the "synopsis" developed in a text, or literary script as it is also known. The word argument comes from the Latin argumetum, it is the summary of a story. Do not confuse these terms. Then, the argument is the summary of the story that we intend to tell in the script; It can have between 5 and 20 pages and must contain the following information:
1 - Temporality
2 - Location
3 - Development of the Action
4 - Character Profile (Protagonist)

Why is an argument made? It is in the argument where you can see the viability of a project. With a ready argument, the production visibilities of the film, art and author industry can be analyzed.

List of Scenes

A very useful practice before writing the script, having already completed the argument; It's the scene list. The list of scenes is a tentative but not definitive notation of the order in which the scenes will be written in the script, without defining even the place or time, but with the action of the characters already established.

It can be divided by the structure of three acts created by Archimedes.

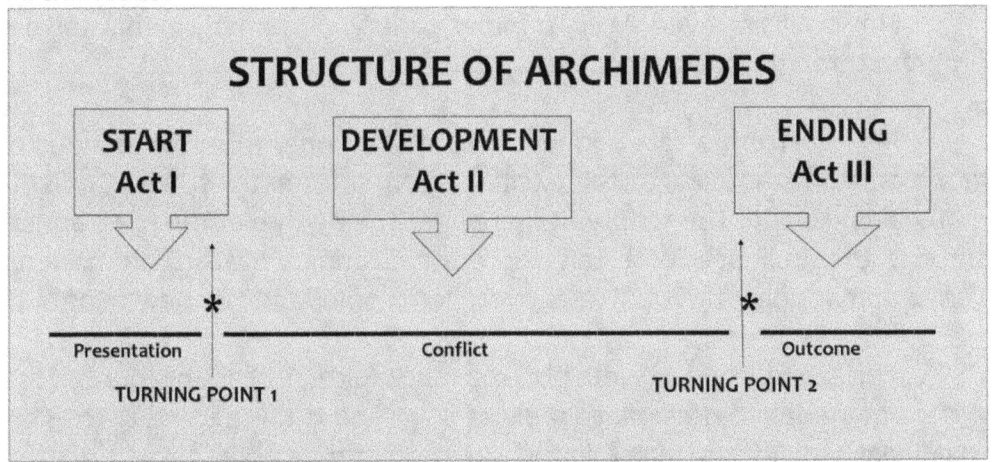

Before writing the script, they should design each program as a visual and auditory experience. They must visualize the total image of what they want to teach, and order the presentation of that information with such rhythm and fluency that they manage to maintain the attention of the public.

At the beginning you will need a hook that naturally captures the viewer's attention. In other words, they will need a powerful, novel, imaginative introduction, etc. to capture the public's attention from start to finish.

Then they will need to tell the story with CONTINUITY, that is, through a series of scenes that carry parts of the story and follow each other with logic, always MOVING the story forward.

TOWARDS THE DISENROLLMENT. The program must end with a PODERSOUS MESSAGE: fast, sharp and memorable, so that the message of the program remains in the public's mind.

Now it is necessary to give emotion to the program. Not only present information during a period of time. This will bore the audience. Instead, the presentation of the information should be designed to awaken or re-engage the audience every few minutes.

How is it achieved? Well, printing variety, o internal rhythm to the program through various segments.

You go from a fast sequence, to a slow one, from live action to graphics, from the dark to the exciting, from information Heavy to light material and so on. The scriptwriter changes the rhythm of the program to surprise the audience. With this you are indicating: "Pay attention, here comes something new" or "This is over, here comes another new thing" ...

For example, if we write about a mechanical process of four pesos. We are not going to present it simply as 1, 2; 3 and 4. It is necessary to alter that linear simplicity to maintain the attention of the public.

This is achieved by designing the program in segments - or recognizable acts -, as in a play. The melting of the music, the narration or the feeling of action tells the audience that the segment has ended. BUT IT IS IMPORTANT TO KEEP AWAY YOUR CURIOSITY ABOUT WHAT COMES AFTER.

Studies indicate that public attention can be "captured" without distractions for up to 8 minutes A short film does not exceed 30 minutes, a medium length has between 30 minutes and 1 hour, and a feature film has more than 1 hour.

ACT 1 o THE HOME

The rule remains the same - a script page equals one minute of screen time. The principle is ACT I, called the preparation, because you have in a script of 120 pages, approximately 30 pages to present your story.

A spectator, in general, goes to the cinema and decides if he "likes" or "does not like" the film. The next time you go to the movies, see how long it took you to decide if the movie you liked or not. It takes about ten minutes, that is, ten pages of the script.

You have to catch the viewer immediately!

You have about ten pages to show the public who is your main character, which are the PREMISES, or PROPOSITIONS that serve as the basis for the plot of the story, and what is the SITUATION.

At the end of the first act there is a DECISIVE POINT: A decisive point is an incident or event that occurs in the story and makes it change in another direction. This event usually occurs between pages 25 and 27.

ACT II o THE CONFRONTATION

Act II contains the bulk of the story. It develops between pages 30 and 90. It is called the confrontation part in the script because the basis of all drama is conflict. Once you have defined the need for your character, that is, discover what you want to achieve during the script, what is your goal, then you can create obstacles to that need, to reach that goal. This generates conflict.

THE DECISIVE POINT: At the end of the second act it usually occurs between pages 85 and 90. This usually leads to the outcome of the story.

Act III: THE UNCONVENTION

It usually occurs between pages 90 and 120. It is the outcome of the story. How it ends? What happens to the main character? Survive or die? Succeeds or fails? A strong ending in the outcome makes the story comprehensible and complete.

All the scripts follow this basic linear structure. The dramatic structure can be defined as: A LINEAR ARRANGEMENT OF INCIDENTS, EPISODES, OR RELATED EVENTS THAT LEAD TO A DRAMATIC OUTPUT.

The way you use these structural components determines the shape of your film.

You can establish a simple formula for the script: It is the description of a person or persons, in a place or places, doing what is 'theirs'. All the scripts have a theme and the theme of the script is defined as action, what happens to the character, to whom it happens.

In the script, the story moves forward, from A to Z, from the preparation to the ending. A LINEAR

ARRANGEMENT OF INCIDENTS, EPISODES, OR RELATED EVENTS THAT LEAD TO A DRAMATIC OUTPUT.

This means that the story moves forward, from beginning to end. They have ten pages to establish three points:

1) Who is the main character,
2) What the story is about, and
3) What are the dramatic circumstances surrounding the story? -

So, what is the best way to start the script? KNOW THE END!
The end is the first thing you should know before you start writing.

Why? It is obvious. Your story always moves forward, it follows a direction, a path, a line of development from beginning to end. You do not have to know the exact ending, but what happens. Good movies always have strong and well-presented endings. A definitive outcome When you know your end it is easy to write the beginning. What is the beginning of the script? As it begins? What do you write after FADE IN:?

If you have determined an ending, you can choose an incident or event that leads to the end. You can present the main character at work, playing, alone or accompanied, whether in business or pleasure. What happens in the first scene? Where it happens?

There are several ways to start a script. You can attrap| to the audience with a visually exciting sequence of action, as in "Star Wars", or you can create an interesting introduction to the character, as in "Shampoo": "A dark room, moans and cries of pleasure. , high, insistent, breaking the mood, is another woman who calls Warren Beatty, who is in bed with Lee Grant, our scene all we need to know about the character.

A start can be visually active and exciting, catching the viewer's attention immediately. Another is more expository, slower pace to establish character and situation. The sequence of the credits is the last thing that is done, and it is a decision of the editor and the director. Whether it's a dynamic montage of credits or just white letters superimposed on a black background, it's not the screenwriter's decision.

The first ten pages are decisive. You have ten pages to catch the public and thirty to present the story.

- Determine the end of the script, and design the principle. the main rule for the start: it will work? in reality does the history in motion? establish the main character?

- Establish the argument (what is the history of)?

- Establish a "problem that the character must confront and overcome? raise the needs of the character?

Dialogged continuity

At the moment of adding scene headings and actions you advance the first steps towards the preliminary script. In order to use the dialogues for storyboarding or to perform a dramatized reading, it is customary to eliminate both headings and descriptions of the action to leave only the dialogues in a continuous way.

The script must be represented very clearly, it is very important because in the production of an audiovisual program it is common to work as a team, which means that the production time is expensive and the mistakes of one person can delay the work of all, it is then convenient to foresee from the beginning that there are no errors due only to the lack of care in the writing or in the way of presenting the script.

TERMS USED IN THE SCRIPT	
SCENIC ADDRESS	Any information describing scene or location, situation, character, technical instructions, very long personal addresses, and a similar one.
CHARACTER	The name, title or description of who says the dialogue.
ACCOMMODATION	Specific and usually short personal instructions for a character in particular, which appear in parentheses just under the name of the character. Examples: (nods), (sits), (trembling with fear).
DIALOGUE	Words spoken by any character. Include what is said when you are "thinking of loud voice ", talking on the phone, or speaking from another room.
SOUND POINT	A sound that requires the technical reproduction services of a sound engineer. The sound notes usually appear in the scenic direction and must be shown in CLOSED CAPS.
CAMERA NOTE	A specific instruction given to the camera. The camera notes appear in the Scenic direction and must also be shown in CAPITAL.
VOIVE OVER	The mechanical transmission of a voice away (V.O.) from the screen, such as a voice in the telephone or a voice on the loudspeaker or a voice on the recorder. It is indicated in VOICE OVER in the scenic direction and (V.o.) next to the character.
OFF SCREEN	A voice or sound heard that comes off screen; off screen, from another room, while the camera focuses on another subject. The person speaking off camera (off screen) is accessible to go on camera. Always abbreviated

LITERARY SCRIPT

It is an ordered narration of the theme of the program or of the story where action and dialogue are included but exempt from any technical indication, the literary script must be used with a television language through "image" and not merely literary.

Some characteristics of the literary script in the writing are:

• The scriptwriter always has to see the narration through images, you must resort to the word when you want to explain something that can not be explained with an action.

• You should not explain the thoughts of the characters in words.

• It is not valid to refer to an action that is not going to happen.

Everything written in the script must be justified in the entire narrative. Beyond the apparent differences imposed by the resource of the different expressions (the combination of image, word and sound on television, the word in literature), the functional and structural dependence that primitive television products had on the literary, it was evident. This fact was later reinforced by an argument of a theoretical nature: both the literary work and the audiovisual products have the same textual nature and, therefore, could and should be studied from the perspectives introduced by the different disciplines that have declared themselves competent in this field. So interdisciplinary object that is the text. The existence of a long literary tradition in the reflection on the problem justified a relationship that, for the rest, could be judged a priori as fruitful.

At present, the first of these reasons has ceased to be operative because, as we will have the opportunity to see later, television products have acquired functions and structural arrangements that are their own. As for the Second, it is subject to a correction derived from a quite evident appreciation: the textual is not identified with the literary. It can not be accurate, therefore, that the reflection on the problem of the genres of television texts has largely dispensed with literary categories.

All this is not an obstacle, however, for us to consider useful some reflections that have arisen in a context such as that of literary theory that has behind it the weight of a long tradition that can not be underestimated.

This tradition has found significant difficulties in establishing sufficiently defined generic classifications. If this fact is taken into account, it could be thought that any attempt to extrapolate the categories that can be used in the literary sphere to the context of television programming will also affect the problems that we have just described. However, if someone comes to believe that the way to avoid such problems is to give up establishing any kind of relationship between both contexts, he would be wrong. The current literary criticism may be conditioned by a rather confused tradition, but its problems have more to do with the difficulties posed by the categorization of a universe of essentially mobile and changing objects than with the literary in the strict sense. Hence, we find ourselves in very similar situations when we try a generic classification of television programming products. Consequently, we should take into account some of the conclusions reached by modern investigations of the problem. More concretely, the following should be considered as pertinent statements:

a) In spite of the epistemological pre-eminence and the recognized exemplary character of the genre with respect to the text, it can rarely be considered as a perfect fulfillment of the text. In other words, the texts do not usually reproduce in their entirety the defining features of the genre, which shows that gender is often more a theoretical category, abstract, than a class defined by induction from the examination of cases .

TECHNICAL SCRIPT

It is the translation in images and sounds of the literary script with all the technical data necessary for the realization of the program, it is what we call technical script. This should be a coordinating document that allows to see the simultaneous and chronological interrelation between dialogue, action and mechanics of the realization.

The technical script contains all the necessary technical descriptions for the director, audio operator, cameramen, set designers, camera operator, editor, floor manager and illuminator.

The technical script describes piano to plan the whole program execution. Some characteristics of the technical script are that the audio column always goes to the right of the page, with all the corresponding details dialogues or comments, environmental noises, music, silences, etc.

THE TELEVISION SCRIPT

Writing a script for television requires a special technique, such as knowing in depth how the so-called "teleplay" is made, it is important to bear in mind that for the elaboration of these scripts it is necessary that the audiovisual producer understands the standard of how it should be to write.

Script format

A script is made up of 7 elements. Each of these is written in a particular way, and its form contains information relevant to the various members of the production team. If a text does not correspond to one of these elements, it must not be in script.

• **Scene Header**

The scene headings describe how the scene will be shot.
The headings are composed of three parts that:
1. Dictate whether the scene will take place inside or outside.
2. Indicate the place where the scene will take place.
3. Show the Time of day when the action will be filmed.

The first element in the header is the abbreviation "EXT.", From the outside, or "INT.", From inside, which indicates whether the action was carried out in the open air or in a closed place.

Sometimes "EXT./INT." Or "I / E" is used to indicate a place that is both an interior and an exterior. For example, a car or the door of a house in which the action contemplates a character outside and another one inside.

The second element of the header is the place where the scene will take place. This information can be general or specific, according to the particular needs of the script.

The last element is the time of day. It is usually specified if it is "DAY" or "NIGHT" since the main use of this information is to define if the scene will be shot day or night. However, when history asks for it, more specific hours can be used such as: "MORNING", "3 AM.", Etc.

When the previous scene and present a continuous action, the time of day is presented with the text "CONTINUOUS". This indicates that it maintains the same Time of Day as the previous scene.

INT. HOUSE - DAY

EXT. HOTEL EMPERADOR - ROOM 507 - NIGHT

EXT./INT. AUTOMOTIVE OF JORGE - CONTINUOUS

A scene header must always be followed by a Description, never by another element of the guide. Nor should it be the last element of a page; When this happens, it should be sent to the next page.

• Description

The Description, also called action, or Direction, consists of paragraphs that describe what the camera sees (and listens to). Consequently,

120

sentences that can not be recorded, such as feelings, intentions, etc., should not be introduced.

The description is always described in the present tense, since it is describing what is happening, omitting redundant references such as "we see" or "it is seen" (since it is understood that if it is written as a description, it is because the camera sees it).

INT. ROOM - NIGHT

Maria enters the room. Look around. His watery eyes. On the bed an old dress. He takes it and caresses it. Spend saliva

Nicolás looks out the door. Maria is startled. Leave the dress on the bed. Blushes.

The paragraphs of the Descriptions are usually short, to facilitate reading.

The text is written in lowercase, except when particular information is presented, which is written in uppercase as:
1. When a character appears for the first time (subsequent times that character appears, it is written in lowercase). This is in order to facilitate the breakdown.
2. When a sound or a sound effect is described.
3. When a camera address is described, such as: PANORAMIC, LOW CAMERA, ANGLE, etc.
4. When describing the text of a message that the public will read on the screen.

Ex.:
FELIPE, a 34-year-old tall man watches as a plane takes off.
The plane passes ON THE CAMERA. It gets lost in the clouds.
Suddenly, the right engine EXPLODES.

Felipe looks at his cell phone. A text message says: "IT'S YOUR FAULT".
Felipe cries.

When we write a sequence for example a car in pursuit, or our protagonist along the avenue, or when a script is blocked, and a new scene is added, it is assigned a new number that identifies it, a letter is added, for example, scene 1, sequence 1A, 1B and 1C. This identifier is formed by the number of the previous scene, followed by the letter.

When a sequence is edited, a letter is added to the beginning so A1A. The pattern indicates that scene A1 precedes scene 1, and after scene 1, follows scene 1. After 1A follow 1B, 1C, etc.

In the filming stage for the continuity control and pre-editing for the post production, the scenes and even the dialogues are numbered. The page number in a dash is placed 18.2 cm from the left edge of the page, already 1.3 cm from the top edge. The page number is immediately followed by a period.

• Character

Before each Dialog block, you must specify which character will interpret it. The character's name must be written in capital letters, aligning (not centered) 10 cm from the edge of the sheet. The name of the character must be constant throughout the script, whether it be a character that changes its name during the story, or that different characters know it by different names. The reason is that this element of the script is aimed at the actor who must memorize the lines, rather than the character. To the right of the character's name, particular marks are sometimes placed in parentheses, which give performance information, and is written in the next row, this is the dialogue dimension.

• Dialogue

The dialogue block indicates the words that the actors will interpret. It is written in lowercase, aligned (not centered), with a left margin of 6.8 cm from the left edge of the page, and a right margin of 6.1 cm from the right edge of the page. sheet. A dialogue should never appear without indicating which character will interpret it. When it is very long, and goes to the next page, mark "MORE" indicating that this dialogue continues on the next page and "CONT'D" at the beginning of the next page. Since Dialogue represents the linguistic patterns of a wide variety of people, it is correct to write them with grammatical errors and colloquialisms. To facilitate reading, the numbers are usually written in words. Each dialogue is a paragraph no matter how long it may be. When a dialogue is interrupted, the "-" symbol is used to indicate that a pause is made at that point in the dialogue. To indicate emphasis on the pronunciation of a word, it is usually underlined.

• Annotation

The dimension or parenthesis, is an element of the script format, intended to give additional information to the form of a dialogue must be said. The instruction is placed in parentheses, aligned 8.6 cm from the edge of the sheet. It is written entirely in lowercase; that is, the first letter is not capitalized, and must be placed between the character and the dialogue, or between paragraphs of the same dialogue.
Dimensions should be used sporadically, and only when necessary.

• Transition

Transitions indicate several methods for moving from one scene to another, such as various types of cuts and dissolvences. These are written in capital letters, aligned 15.2 cm from the left edge of the page. The exception is the "FADE IN:", which is usually placed to indicate the beginning of a script. This transition is tabulated to 4.3 cm. The transitions end in two points ":" when they indicate a relation with the next scene, and in point "." When they do not have it. In the past, when a scene ended, the transition "CUT TO:" was marked before starting the next one.

However, the Scene Header that is not preceded by a transition has an implied "CUT TO:", so today it is not used much but to mark a change of place and important time. However, it is still seen in some scenes, when a writer wants to give him a certain score at the end of a sequence of scenes. A transition should never start a page. When this happens, a portion of the description or Dialogue that precedes it, should be moved to the new page.

• Flat

The plane is the element that indicates a direction instruction. It is used to highlight that a particular cinematographic plane is fundamental for the story. Since the choice of the planes is a function of the director and not of the scriptwriter, this element should be used sparingly. The plane is written in two parts: The subject is separated from the plane of action in two different lines. The line describing the subject is capitalized, and the line describing the action is in lowercase. But despite being divided into two lines, at the level of punctuation, it is treated as if it were a single sentence.

Script software

Until the year 2012 precise measures were used for the script format, today it is enough to download a script editor from the Internet. A script program or package for scripts, such as Celtx and others like Dramatica, takes all the hard work and offers a range of options to manage your storyboard and script in the easiest way, these are generally recognized for their weight in gold .

You could be hindered by their prices and payment methods, but most people spend more on hobbies, games and dvd. If you are willing to try them, you could aspire to present them to an executive at a price of $ 15,000.00 and more.

The Preliminary Screenplay

Up to here you have been able to land your idea enough to decide to at least take paper and pen to write down your first ideas, towards a real and tangible script. It is important to keep enthusiasm up at this stage, and set realistic goals, such as a daily script page. This does not sound like many, but as in the fable of the hare and the turtle, you will finish and you will not be left behind on the way.

A typical screenwriter often regrets that after starting a few first pages for a week, then they fall into a pond and leave the habit for a few days and then forget it completely. Be regular, constant, let the writing be your guide.

First script outline

Now that you have the first written draft, take a break and we want to say a real break away from home. Go to the movies, play games, read magazines, go out with your friends and do whatever you want, but think about your script. A couple of days later, pick up your script and make a first reading from start to finish. Ask yourself, were there any problems in the jumps that left you lost? Did you find any inconclusive holes in your story? No problem, make a second reading on your print and make notes where you think there are flaws, not only grammar but also format.

Re-write your draft and find opinions

Sit another day and reincorporate those improvements or changes you were thinking about. If you have some reader friends in whose opinion you trust, they are intelligent and cinephile and can be impartial when commenting on your work, then it is time to show them to them to read and perfect your masterpiece. Give them a reasonable time to let you know their thoughts, do not be anxious asking them every day if they have already read it. Once they have given you their opinion, remember that it is not mandatory to incorporate everything they say, each person has their point of view, just listen to them and assume to add what they have agreement with you.

Get professional help

We are not referring to a psychiatrist, which may come after you have trouble getting over the idea that the collection report is less than you expected. We want to say a professional who reads your script, someone who reads every day and knows what works and what does not, why and more important than everything, how to adjust it.

We do that work in our city to live and that is why we dare to suggest these tips. Not only for us but also for the local film industry. Many style correctors offer a regular commission and pass a report of your analysis with all the suggestions and ideas to adjust the final version of your script. Of course they will try to make necessary changes, but the agents in the industry are not stupid and if you contact them for a second chance they will remember that they rejected your script. Look for other options a lot of writers who together form a remarkable network. The trick here is to change the initial title by one that highlights those changes, and remember the industry professionals are not fools.

Last rewrite of your script

Gather all the notes and advice you have received from friends, professional proofreaders and others and do a small rewrite of the beginning of your script. This final version of your script must be fuller, much more interesting and with better rhythm than before as a result. Read it again and you'll see that it reads like a real script, like a real movie! Do not make changes just on a whim, it only incorporates those that make the story go forward.

Send it out

This is the final step that can take you to get the representation of a sales agent, probably by the type of optional or percentage agreement. An agent does not come easy, at least the best of them. Check the options in your locality to get an agent in an international forum, a responsible state office or in independent film schools. This will not be a simple task, if it were everyone would be a writer, but it is possible if you trust that you have written something very good; It will be much easier for you.

An agent has contacts within the industry that can turn your script into a movie, he knows studio executives and production companies as well as independents. They will act as your link and if someone is interested in signing you will be notified, in return they must obtain a commission percentage on the sale of at least 10%.

Another way is the contests, if you stay alert to find out about the calls, fill the requirements and you send your script, television or film, you can bet that the agents will not be far from considering it. This seems more difficult than it is, but you can send your script to everyone you want, there are registration rules so that outside of them
your shipment can be returned. Do not try it out of time since surely the copy of your work may end up in the dumpster, since they are not willing to waste time.

This system works thanks to the audiovisual industry does not stop, and could at any time resume a search that closes in a few months without maximum publicity, they are inside and outside. Here is the secret, the international industry is very aware of the changing role of the Internet to acquire scripts, they do not wait for projects that come to them, they can find them when they want. They no longer receive them like that, because their offices would be filled with envelopes and packages containing scripts they will never be able to read. That is a legal nightmare.

Sometimes the Internet facilitates this process by receiving by email to its servers, without the need to print for what it is known of the open formats of texts or pdf.

The 6 questions

For months, or perhaps years, you have focused your passion and energy on the culmination of your script. Put your heart and soul into your characters and their conflicts. You have read and reviewed the grammar. You have given it to friends or colleagues who expressed their opinion about it. And they loved him. But is your script ready?

Look at it one last time and ask yourself this vital question: Does it smell my script to a movie? Believe me, producers, agents, directors, stars and executives know a movie once they have read it. They can suspect it. They may not be able to describe to you why a script is ready to be a movie, that just happens.

There is a simple list of six points that will help you develop your own sense of smell. Here it is:

1. Who?
2. Want what?
3. Where?
4. When?
5. Why?
6. How?

If your script answers the following questions, then it is probably ready for the market.

1. THE QUESTION OF THE WHO - ABOUT WHO IS THE MOVIE?

This is the first question that a producer asks himself. There is only one correct answer; the movie has to be about the star protagonist. Movies usually focus on the protagonist - a hero who must overcome difficulties, sometimes impossible obstacles, to pursue what he wants. The audience must feel wrapped up in this hero and his challenge. If you are not sure which of your characters is the star of your movie; Then your script is not ready for the film industry. What is your audience or target of your movie? That is the second question that a financial partner will ask you after reading your script. Get to know your audience Many movies cross two genres of audiences at once, but your script must be able to attract at least one defined market.

2. THE QUESTION OF WHAT: WHAT WENT?

What are the movie markets? You can invent your story for your favorite market, just make sure you have one of these in your script. Writing movies is telling stories. The movies are promoted as comedies, dramas, action and so on. Know the genre of your movie. The most popular are: Comedy Drama, Animation and Family, Romance, Urban, Action, Adventure, Fantasy, Science Fiction, Thriller, War and Terror. Your movie can combine two genres, but if your script mixes more than three, you must rethink your movie. Find out what the movies in your genre have done, the successful ones and the ones that failed. This way of thinking will help you stand out in your gender.

Imagine a poster for your movie or imagine the trailer that will announce your movie, if you can not do it ask yourself: Why not?

3. THE QUESTION OF WHERE: YOUR SOLE WORLD

A successful movie script should give the reader a unique sense of place, it is the cosmos of the movie. Art directors, set designers, directors, and photography contribute immensely to the appearance of the film. But a well written script puts its characters in a single space created by the writers with words. We recommend reading movie scripts such as: The Lord of the Rings, The Cat in the Hat, Private Ryan, Anaconda and observe the descriptions of place and sounds to observe differences to choose the environment of your script.

4. THE QUESTION OF WHEN: ESTABLISH TIME

Your film will be developed at a point in the past, like the second world war in "The Labyrinth of the Faun" by Guillermo del Toro or "Titanic" by James Cameron, or at a point in the present as the most recent documentary, or in the future as the latest sequel to "Stars Wars" or "Avatar." The peplum is the cinematographic genre that encloses history and Science Fiction futurism. The period in which your film is located is emphasized throughout the script?

If a computer appears in your scene of the Russian revolution it could be an error or unforgivable anachronism, mixtures of Greek myth and youthful drama as in "Percy Jackson" must have certain dramatic rules.

5. THE QUESTION OF HOW: TECHNIQUE AND RHYTHM

The films build their own narrative rhythm through the description of the action, camera techniques, use of visual and sound effects, unforgettable dialogues and the juxtaposition of scenes.

There is a subliminal map of emotions that excite us, depress us, indignant us, surprise us and in the end we are passionate about them. When producers, screenwriters and fundraisers read your script and discover your character's emotions, they will at least have discovered your ability to instill rhythm into your movie. Do your character's actions illuminate your character's decisions? Do you use gestures, camera movements and other tools to get closer to your hero?

6. THE QUESTION OF WHY: DO IT AND SEE IT

Why would a film or television director or scriptwriter spend a year of his life preparing and making this film? Why is your character attractive? Why would a study, the local government or an entrepreneur invest money in your script? Why would spectators pay the entrance to the movie theater? In the sale of a script the six questions are perhaps the most important to consider, although also the most ephemeral ones. Why would someone buy your script? When you manage to answer these questions you will know that your script is ready for the industry.

Legal Management in development

If your idea is original, there is no problem, just write it, the ideas that originate in you bring their own rights. If your idea is like resources 2 or 3, you will have to make sure that you have the right to use rights. As a general rule, all works written before 1923 are in the public domain, which means that you do not have to ask permission from the copyright holder. Works published after 1923, but before 1978, are protected for 95 years from the date of publication. Works published after 1978, are protected for life more than 70 years after the death of the author. So to make sure that the work is free it is suggested to call the Copyright Registration Office of your locality to request.

For articles you can contact journalists directly from the press. In some countries like Panama, the term of rights after the death of the author is 50 years.

When the idea comes from a public figure or recent historical figure this is a private person, then you have to contact your heirs, if this person is no longer alive, and sign an agreement with them for the rights of your

authorized biography. Although this is not always required, this will be a gesture that your heirs will appreciate before seeing the story on the big screen. This will also inform us if these rights have already been transferred to other producers, but you can shoot a version of the facts in the life of the celebrity. To ensure legal protection, you should contact a lawyer who mediates between the parties when someone shows interest in producing the script.

When dealing with a public figure, care must be taken not to write a defamatory event or reveal any privacy of your life that may be considered an invasion of privacy. If your character is very historical, you are lucky because historical events can not be recorded, just make sure you write a very personal story as a version or interpretation that does not resemble those of other authors.

This was the general rule of thumb, but it does not hurt to seek additional legal advice. So take your idea and make it run, that's how the writing process begins.

Types of works assignment agreements

The cinema is a venture, therefore planning is essential. The Legislation for the promotion of audiovisuals are taken according to each country. In Panama, Law 16 of 2010 is the legal framework to direct our production strategy.

Author Registration It must be reviewed and negotiated among the project representatives.

RECRUITMENT:

In co-production contracts you have to have a company and not take the contract as definitive, this is for the number of sections. It is recommended a process without formalities, avoiding people who do not want to sign.

Everything must be done without haste or pressure.

Regarding government subsidies, the amounts enter the company's account, and not the producer's personal account. The assets of each one must be separated.

There are two types of agreement of assignment of ideas, arguments, scripts, etc. in the audiovisual industry:

1. Optional agreement: means that you, the writer, will give an exclusive authorization to a production company or producer to try to establish the financing and turn your script into a movie. The optional agreement will specify the final sales price of your script or a percentage of the future collection, with the period of time that the producer will have to gather the funds or otherwise his license will expire, which can range from six months to 2 years. . The sum of money or offer changes, can be up to $ 1 to $ 5,000 or more, but the idea is to keep your eyes on how much your script will actually sell.

2. Agreement for release: it implies only the reading of the script and a signature releasing of responsibility to the producers of demands if a similar idea is released.

The standard pattern of the script format is easy to learn and is what the executives expect from you to get it and they will not consider you if you can not. After all, if you do not achieve this basic format correctly, what impression will the rest of the script give you?

Some aspects of formatting are rules and others are guides to be the first and to stay later and continue with the triumphant combination. Know the difference between a participation and a shoot. Many of the scripts that will be read by the producers are filming and have camera addresses, scene numbers, etc. Your script should not carry them, since they should pass into the hands of a director and you should not tell them how to do their work.

COVER OF THE SCRIPT: This is the first page of your script and you must identify your contact information or that of your agent. It is all you need.
- The title of your movie.
- Your name.
- Your address
- Your phone number and email
- Copyright registration number.

ESTIMATED PRICE:

A famous screenwriter made this concept of negotiating and including it famous, if you decide to do it, you will look like a beginner who will find it quite difficult. This Hollywood screenwriter is Shane Black and has the record of having sold all his scripts above $ million per script, and in fact his masterpiece "A long Kiss Goodnight" cost 4 million.

EXTENSION OF THE SCRIPT:

Start by writing a short film of no more than 30 pages, with its introduction of characters, conflict and resolution.

This should be your first challenge as an aspiring screenwriter or audiovisual professional as it will help you understand how an effective shooting will work. If your inspiration is fluid, try adapting to stories, plays or short novels, do not dare to adapt extensive works of more than 300 pages, it is not for a beginner to be encouraged. Once you have practiced a little, give free rein to your idea of a feature film that should be 120 pages, and at 100 if it is comedy. There must be a balance between dialogues and descriptions, nor should there be scenes of more than three pages of repetitive, absurd or out-of-topic dialogue.

It is important to remember that the industry is ambiguous, if an executive reads your script and it seems good it does not mean that the collection of financing will be prompt, if another executive says it is bad, it does not mean that another does not seem to give you an opportunity. Many of the best screenplays were rejected for various reasons, and then they became great movies thanks to the intervention of talented staff. Allow this to be a collaborative process.

Types of Contracts

As a writer, you will find many types of contracts throughout your career. It is valuable to have prior knowledge of such contracts, in order to be prepared and act informed. The film industry is a dream factory and ignorance is not rewarded here.

A good start is to start with the author registration in your local office, with this certification most of the contracts and basic clauses are going to be established. The idea is to negotiate something better and use this as the path to the contract of your dreams. Identify your priorities and you will know which points are negotiable and which are not.

Here are the four types of basic contracts you will find:

- **Option Agreement**: A purchase option will give the producer, within a limited period of time, the right to buy your script through other interested parties, for which they will pay a fixed amount, ranging from $ 1 to a few Dollars.

For example, you can sign an optional 12-month agreement for $ 1,000. After twelve months, if the producer has not been able to shoot the film and you do not want to extend the agreement any longer, you keep the $ 1,000. The agreement will detail not only the terms, but also the final or percentage purchase price, so it must be read carefully before signing to be successful in the future. An option agreement is necessary for the producer, so you do not waste time planning your project with Study A, only to find out that the script has been sold to Estudio B. It is important to respect the option period of the person who maintains it and trust that You will have the ability and the contacts to take out your film, because this will be blocked for any other until the license expires.

- Purchase contract: This is really the sale of the script and the buyer will acquire all the economic and representation rights, the only moral right that will be maintained is to mention the original authorship. In addition, a percentage of the gross collection may be received if it is produced. If a purchase contract emerges suddenly, legal advice should be sought immediately and the documentation of the proposal carefully reviewed.

- **Oral Contract**: An oral agreement allows a producer to negotiate a deal around your script. Unlike an optional agreement, nothing is signed and there is no money involved, however it does not mean that there is nothing written on paper. It is a good idea to follow meetings by phone, through which the terms are discussed, with letters, faxes or e-mails until the moment you have a coherent paper and both parties know what is acceptable and what is not for the future development of the script. Oral contracts may not lead anywhere, but allow you to establish relationships and open up possibilities for future projects.

- Writing assignment: It can be the writer's shrimp. The trick is that you will need to have at least one script produced under your pocket, to be considered for such work. This speaks less than real talent and more than an easy sale to an investor. This is not a quick or hard rule, and many agents will use a copy of a script there to get an assignment based on their strengths. These writing assignments cover jobs such as rewriting and formatting the work that someone else wrote. An assignment memo will outline the specifics of what should be written, when it should be ready and for what compensation. There is a payment or partial payment, with the recorderis to complete the delivery. Although it does not require a long negotiation, it is always valuable to look at the details, but keep it pleasant so that the work is completed.

The Screenwriter and the producer

In the case of the Writer-Producer: This relationship should be arranged very well. In cases where there are two writers without a contract, it is demanded and if it is won; A cost is paid.

Between the Writer and the Producer the following is taken into account:
- The type of verbal contract should be left aside.

- They should know that they can start a business.
- There must be signed authorizations from each party.
- We must respect the original credit of the authors and not forget it.
- There is plagiarism when the characteristics of the text or image are obvious. Example "Claus case" for illegitimate use of images.

Regarding the "public domain" of some classic works, the status of the work must be verified since the heirs of the author seek mechanisms so that these author rights do not expire when the period after death is over. Example:

Mickey Mouse, The Little Prince.

Agreements between co-authors are by percentage of participation or number of pages of the original or adapted script.

KEY IDEAS OF THIS CHAPTER

▶The script is the fundamental pillar of any audio-visual project, be it a simple block structure and breaks commercial, that is, this literary with precise descriptions and dialogues.

▶The technical script and the storyboard are essential tools for the staff when shooting a film, be it a short film, half-length or full-length film, animated or with Effects. We should never avoid them because of the fact feel ourselves already experts in the matter, or for lack of sufficient previous time. When we are beginners we must Plan, compare and improve the documents as much as possible before starting the shoot.

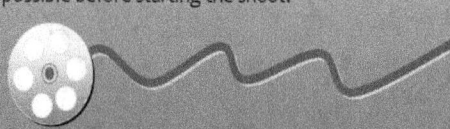

1. ▶An idea goes through several stages. It is not difficult to start immediately with a script editor program and

get later a plan of automatic shooting, but start with a simple synopsis, its treatment, and a list of scenes facilitates creative work during development or pre-production.

SUGGESTED ACTIVITIES

1. Carry out the development of your project:
2. Choose a teleplay format or movie script.
3. Write a synopsis, its treatment and a list of scenes, in a maximum period of one month.
4. Design the profile of characters: protagonists, secondary and incidental.
5. Aim to write between 1 and 5 daily pages of film script or TV series as a long-term plan.

CHAPTER 6

PREPRODUCTION

- ▶ Pre-Production Organization
- ▶ Legal management in Preproduction
- ▶ Artistic Direction
- ▶ Page To page
- ▶ Storyboarding
- ▶ Teaser
- ▶ Financing and Co-production
- ▶ The Picht
- ▶ Location Scouting ▶ Castings
- ▶ Filming Plan   ▶ Acting Coach

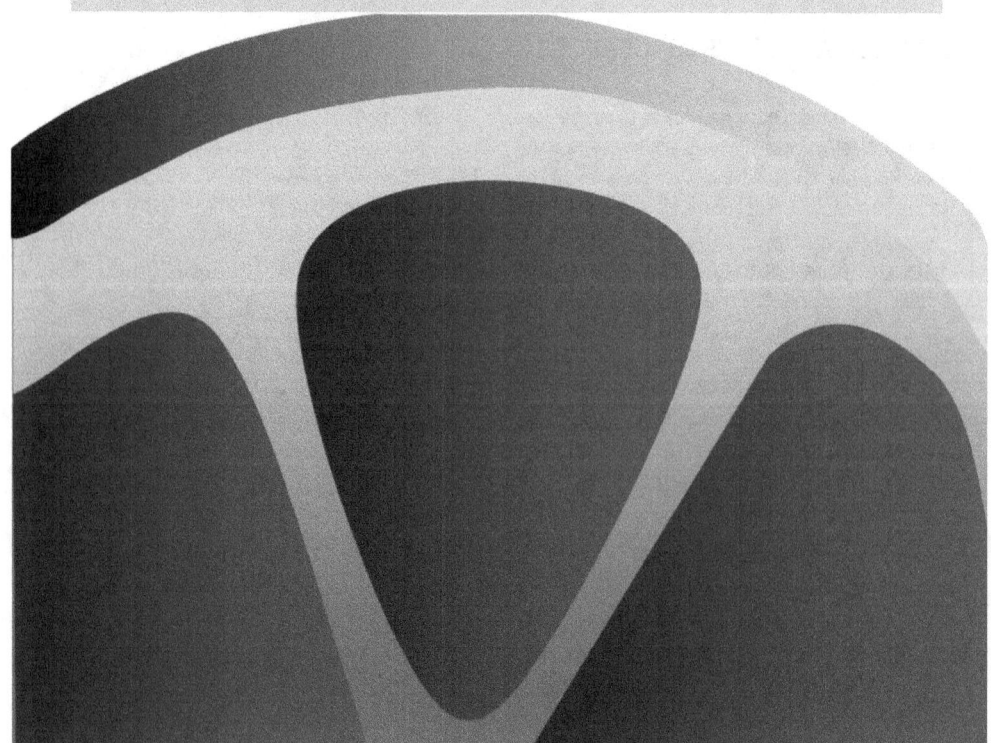

Pre Production

What comes after the script? Bringing the idea of a screenwriter to reality is an arduous project, which demands planning and execution of activities and tasks from short to very long term. Pre-production is a stage of addition importance before starting an audiovisual shoot, since that's when you choose financial partners, personal artistic and managerial, locations, costumes and other elements that will create the unique atmosphere that we want to give to our movie Everything must be ready to comply with a strict Tax Drafting Plan that will be based on a budget exact.

In the execution of the Pre-production plan it will be necessary to identify the problems that can both advance and delay the project, and try to solve them.

The requirements of technical and artistic resources generated by the project will be analyzed to ensure that nobody is overloaded to carry out their task.

Pre-Production Organization

Pre-Production is the whole process prior to recording or filming, in this case, of your audiovisual project. Through this course you will be able to become a television producer in the genre you desire.

A. Stages in the Pre-Production

The Pre Production consists of several stages that are listed below:

1. The search for ideas: It is considered that this sub-stage of pre-production is very important because it is the basis of the entire production process.

2. Research: This stage is of equal importance as the basic idea because it is at this stage that this idea can be changed by another, if we notice that its viability of production does not proceed. Research is important because it is the basis of the production that you will develop and it will determine the veracity of the information that you will assign to your audience or target.

3. The Budget: The budget is an estimate, in money how much it will cost to transcribe your script in audio and video. You can not advance your project without structuring a budget, it will depend on the following sub-stages of the pre-production process and production and post-production. At this time, perhaps you should evaluate your idea and make it simpler and therefore accessible with a low budget. This concept covers amounts from $ 100 to half a million.

4. Legal advice: It refers to the activities prior to filming, such as the preparation of a budget, planning and other preparations. The preproduction period can last a month in the case of a movie, or only a week if it is an episode for a television comedy.

More complex productions, such as tele-marathons or live award ceremonies, may require months of pre-production. The three key people in this process are the production manager, the director and the casting or casting director. The production manager must, first of all, make a provisional budget, hire a manager of locations and heads for the different departments. The first essential decisions for production are the location for the filming and the start date of it. The director reviews the script and makes the changes he considers necessary, begins the casting or casting selection process and chooses his assistants and camera operators. From this moment all decisions related to the cast, creative staff, locations, schedules or visual components must have the approval of the director.

The pre-production process continues with a main meeting or "page to page" attended by all team members, producers, the director and often also the scriptwriter. The pre-production team, conducted by the director, reviews each scene of the script in detail. Each element of the production is analyzed and the questions that may arise are answered. The duration of the meeting may vary, depending on the complexity of the production, from two hours to a whole day.

Legal management in Preproduction

For the legal diligence of collecting the documents required to prove the originality of the original script version and the story, the services of a lawyer will be available. This will be responsible for publicly verifying the relationship agreements of the organization between the Writer-director and the Producer.

LIMITED COMPANY AND LEGAL RIGHTS.

The organization of the film will be formed as a Limited Liability Company LLC.

- Limited liability company, is a type of commercial company in which the capital, which is divided into social participations, is made up of the contributions of all the partners, who do not respond personally to the social debts.

The denomination must include the indication 'Limited Company' or the 'abbreviations SRL or SL It shall have a minimum share capital - lower than that required for the incorporation of public limited companies - which is

divided into indivisible and accumulable social participations, which do not have the securities can not be represented by means of securities or book entries, or called shares.The SL can not agree or guarantee the issuance of obligations.The incorporation of companies will be made by public deed registered in the Commercial Registry, with which it acquires its legal personality.The constitution deed expresses the identity of the members, the contributions made and the shares assigned in payment, the statutes, the way in which the administration is organized and who the administrators are. Bylaws shall include at least the name of the company, the object, address and share capital, the closing date of the fiscal year and the way of organizing the administration of the company. They can be contributed or rights, but not work or services; the contributions can be monetary and not monetary. It is possible to agree accessory services as well as the transmission of the social participations, which will be recorded in the register of partners, transmission that can be inter vivos and mortis causa.

- ORGANS OF THE COMPANY.

There are special rules regarding the form and content of the call, place of celebration, attendance and representation, general meeting table, right of information, conflict of interest and majority principle game, and the record in the minutes of the social agreements.

- There will be a notarial deed of the general meeting and the possibility of challenging social agreements. The administration of the company can be entrusted to a single administrator, to several administrators who act jointly or jointly, or to a board of directors. In the latter case, the bylaws or, failing that, the general meeting will set the minimum and maximum number of its components and the system of organization and operation, a system that must include in all cases the convening and constitution rules of this body, as well as the way to deliberate and adopt agreements. There are special rules regarding the following issues: appointment of administrators, alternate administrators, duration and performance of the position, representation of the company and its scope, separation and responsibility of the administrators.

Project Producer Rights

The partner that welcomes to represent the project of producing the adapted film, is responsible for fulfilling the assignments that compete and managing the financial resources obtained in a reliable manner.
- He is responsible for turning an idea into a movie.
- Responsible for finding funding for the project, bringing together people capable of making the film, and finally, getting agreements for the distribution and exhibition of the finished product.
- By pre-legal condition, you already share with the scriptwriter / director the distribution rights that you will contract after the realization. Both will decide the actors for the cast with the casting director.
- Once the financing is obtained through private partners or investors, a limited company is constituted.
- The producer is usually the main responsible for it, or the partner that controls it. If deemed appropriate, the production company will subaltern certain functions by hiring a representative, called the executive producer, who will be aware of the production and controlling its entire process.
- Finally, the person or persons who contribute financially to the making of a film receive the name of associated producers or another similar one.

Contracts for co-production

Executive co-producers (International) Projects must establish a professional and fraternal bond with producers of leading companies in the field of filmmaking. The guidelines are usually a pre-sale for a reasonable cost in exchange for the ticket office of a country where the associate producer operates. A lawyer licensed in the area of civil and commercial rights must mediate in the signing of this co-production contract.

This is also to comply with the guidelines of the financial subsidy contracts of the sponsoring bodies of regional and European countries that are expected to be carried out.

Social Rights of employees

In co-production contracts you have to have a company and not take the contract as definitive, this is for the number of sections. It is recommended a process without formalities, avoiding people who do not want to sign.

Everything must be done without haste or pressure.

The members of the organization will recognize the social rights of the people hired according to the time and place they participate in the feature film project.
- · Medical assistance insurance for Writer-Director.
- · Producer medical assistance insurance.
- · Medical assistance insurance for managerial / artistic personnel and production assistants.

Musicalization Rights or Soundtrack

In this project a musician will be hired who will be in charge of composing the musical pieces that will be used in the final edition of the scenes of the film, signing his authorization. Normally, it emphasizes the main title and credits of a film, while incidental music is used throughout the film for dramatic purposes. The soundtracks also contain live music, justified in the image by the presence of radio sets, turntables or live musicians. It is usually composed after having made the final editing of the film in order to achieve a perfect synchronization between the action and the music. The composer watches the film already assembled in the company of the director, with whom he discusses the location and style of each musical fragment. Then you are provided with a video tape of this montage, with the built-in time code or sheets with the marked times, from which to work. The final result is recorded in a studio while passing the movie at the same time; thus, recordings are obtained which are then mounted, mixed and transferred to magnetic or optical support, now in disuse, due to digital audio recording and measuring devices.

Artistic Direction

The production company that will represent us will be responsible for arranging a person inside your company to perform all the functions of office assistance and communication with the partners of this artistic and commercial organization.

DIRECTOR OF PHOTOGRAPHY. A professional with experience in handling film camera photography, formats and other necessary equipment will be contacted to verify the costs of realization.

ARTISTIC DIRECTORS. Two professionals with experience in artistic management will be contacted for the design of interiors, of the characters and in the case of animation that are in accordance with the vision of the film.

Designers are able to create compelling scenarios using facades with appearances of solid brick buildings. The second will emphasize that the profile of each character and their movements are met as the necessary technique to achieve it.

The artistic director of a production or animator is the person responsible for the design of the sets and the overall appearance of the film. In films where costumes are an essential part of the story, as in period films, the costume designer (costume designer) becomes another key member of the production team. Other essential designers are those who deal with graphic design of special effects and other visual aspects of production.

As well as a casting director for the selection of the cast of actors for the recording of key voices and movements in the interior studio.

Page to page

The page to page or "page to page" is a reading and review of the script prior to filming that is done in a round table with all the directors of a film or television project. In this pre-production process the Producer will make the first reading of the final script of the film and together with the production assistant will mark with their respective color or sign for the distribution of the elements of the production. With this, each technical and artistic director will be able to start programming according to the requirements of each scene.

This Structural Breakdown Script will be used:

1. The director: will articulate his staging as it is a plot realization;
2. The interpreters will have it to analyze the character of the characters that correspond to them and to know the dialogues.
3. The production manager will have it to develop a coherent work plan;
4. The director of photography, to imagine the chromatic climates and establish the technical means that will be necessary to achieve them; for any other question or confusion about the description of how a sequence occurs.
5. The artistic director is in charge of selecting the environments or building the required sets;

6. The tailor or costume designer is required to make or adapt the essential clothing;

7. The sound manager will have the script to define the character of the soundtrack and its equipment;

8. The editor or editor will have the script to guide the ordering of the shots as they are made and processed;

9. The administrator, to organize the flow of expenses. On a time scale, it is programmed how the budget money is going to be spent: Actors, Extras, Special Effects, Special Equipment, Props, Vehicles and animals and Sound Effects.

It is divided into two phases:

a) The "Storm of Ideas" meeting in which, with the presence and opinion of the Directors and Heads of Production, each of the scenes and their sequences is analyzed from beginning to end so that their elements can be analyzed and reduced in several lists of guides.

b) Listings: These lists will be written by the respective directors or heads of each artistic area to guide their assistants. They are programmed to establish the exact and balanced production budget, avoiding over-costs. The artistic director designs the artistic patterns for the heads of lighting, costumes, makeup and special effects; based on the theme, dramatic turns and conflicts between the characters in the script.

Storyboarding

With the isolation of each scene of the final script, that is, eliminating or correcting the final details of the project, each of the scenes is listed to establish the shooting plan. The illustrations drawn in frames of sequences are made for the purpose of pre-visualizing each frame of the sequence. Its purpose is to order the succession of assembly units that are the planes and set their duration.

It is used to determine in which parts special requirements of the budget arise as they are carried out in studies or abroad. As options for this process of storyboarding can be done only with master scenes, develop the complete film or not done in the case of having an obstacle or setback.

A storyboarding sheet is divided into three pictures and characters are drawn, framing, duration in seconds, dialogue guide and any additional annotation that is considered important.

Regularly in black and white, but color can be added in case of 2D or 3D animations. It can be abstained from being carried out only when it is considered that the complexity of the script does not represent greater camera indications or special or mechanical effects.

Teaser

In the search for timely financing, some of the producers of a film, and due to the need to sell their idea to possible financial partners, and professionals in the film industry, have proposed as a requirement the presentation of a teaser attached to the portfolio of all project.

A "teaser" video means trying tentatively how the project would look if it were to be produced, which would be its environment, by showing a location in a few moments, of no more than a minute. It is not necessary to show actors but to leave some text or speech that describes the synopsis or essence of their argument.

Location Scouting

Based on the list of scene headings described in the final version of the script, we carry out a search of the locations that most resemble the descriptions and environment of our film. The Internet can be a useful tool when consulting places to rent where most scenes occur. However, in order to reduce production costs, it is customary to request farms belonging to friends who are part of the team, here the assistant director has a very important work since it is possible that it has to be shot in two locations at the same time.

Among the recommendations made during the scouting are:

- · Bring a camera or video recorder and record the precise spaces where each scene could be shot.
- · The sources of electricity must be taken into account, since it is also usually provided with its own power plant to avoid possible delays.
- · The sound also considered in case of rain that types of roofs cover the structure, if there are animals nearby, if there is wind or if it will be necessary to isolate the sound doors.
- · Occasionally there are no sanitary toilets and it is necessary to foresee any situation for the needs of the staff when it is rolling.
- · If production requires special make-up, it is essential to separate a dressing room area for the actors to arrange each scene beforehand.
- · The use permits requested to the local authorities for filming in parks or public areas must be requested in advance for the filming dates, since the authorizations take time to leave.
- · Print your selected location images and place them on a mural in your office for later reference of your work team.
- · Suggest, if necessary, color changes of walls and furniture that the decoration manager has requested to the production.

The Picht

The picht is a concept used in the search stage for the completion of any project, whether it has anything or part of the budget. In this the following aspects are taken into account:

- · Who I am?
- · What producer do I represent?
- · What is a project? Mention your synopsis and genres.
- · Elements of production: actors, who does what, where will the funds be obtained?

We must be convinced of our disposition and capacity, not include camera movements and use music that goes according to the theme of our film in the teaser.

Financing and Co-production

The budget approach must always be confronted with the technique to be used during filming. When a relationship between partners is established with the budget, there are cases in which the launch is not included for the post-production budget because it is the producer's own account. The main task in co-production is to establish the percentages between most and less in terms of gross collection when the film is released.

We must look at it in one of these two ways: Either you make the budget for the movie or the movie for the budget.

Everything indicates that we must go out and look for the quotes of each detail of the budget to know how much they charge in each service in which it will be spent. The main thing is to adapt to the budget category of each film project. We take into account whether it is a microenterprise, small or medium-sized company, or class B.

It is said that "In the viability of production, cost is the first factor to be considered."

To get an idea of production costs, a low-budget Latin American film can opt for state or regional funds that are around the quarter of a million dollars as the largest financial source. While a television series composed of 20 episodes, approximately US $ 300,000.00 is US $ 15,000 per episode. Then we can imagine the severity that will be in the choice of a project to film, taking into account that any film is an investment made by a producer, whose purpose is commercial gain.

However, in general, the producer tends to exaggerate the cost of a production to the extent that, for example, to film a battle, he only manages to think of reproducing a battle as it would be in reality instead of thinking about create the illusion of battle.

So, in reproduction, the costs are enormous. And they denote the inability to imagine a creative solution and at a lower cost.

In his film Gaijim, Tisuka, the brilliant Brazilian filmmaker, created a battle scene, using only a cloud of sand, a Japanese in a float and a shattered flag. However, the battle was there. As we see, the costs may vary according to the director's creativity.

In the market viability, it is necessary to analyze if there is an audience for the show and what that public represents in economic terms. A high-cost film but with a small audience will usually find it more difficult to be produced. If we segmented the North American, Asian and Latin American markets separately, we found many differences in production costs and collection probabilities.

Of course, for every rule there are exceptions and sometimes a producer bets on a film without great commercial expectations and the film ends up being a blockbuster, cases like these are "Paranormal Activity", "La Virgen de los Sicarios" and " The Blair Wicht Project ".

In the same way that a film can be produced with all the possibilities of being a success and it turns out to be a fiasco like "Modzila". They are risks of the trade, the risks of a producer. Personally, I think there is an audience for any show. It is said that from a well told story nobody escapes.

In the artistic viability, we will have to investigate if we have available technical personnel and actors capable of satisfactorily performing certain roles for the economic offer that we are able to offer, is what currently becomes the dilemma of the growing and unprofitable audiovisual industry.

As is known, in Latin America there was great difficulty in finding complete actors, but now it is more competitive, besides representing, they can dance, sing, etc. A constant complaint from the directors is the lack of technical personnel such as cameramen, makeup artists or cinematographers.

We know, however, that these deficiencies are determined by the same lack of film course, or acting coach who intends to train actors and technicians, both for television and for film and theater. But this lack is emphasized by the absence of creative projects and the intermittent capacity of governments and private companies to support and finance these proposals. It begins in a system that gives the population some basic conditions of development, but that is not yet integrated collaboratively to guarantee its survival.

On the one hand there is the marked interest of governments to take advantage of the facilities offered to international producers who see in tourist destinations the ideal locations to shoot their films with ambitiously commercial arguments. And on the other hand, we see the documentary makers moved by projecting through their lenses the injustices, tragedies and idiosyncrasies of those who lack housing, food, education; in short, all those things that are lacking between each generation and individual to fully develop their potential.

A typical case is the almost nonexistence of black actors in Latin America. The middle class is basically composed of whites, if we can talk about skin color in a mestizo country like ours. Either way, we know that the middle class is composed mostly of descendants of colonizers and European immigrants, therefore white, where the income is high enough to allow access to education, good food, etc.

Finally, we have authorial viability. For the series industry and television novels, we have to consider three factors.

1. If the argument is for a mega production that can be developed in, let's say 100 chapters, or on the contrary it is an argument that has budget and content only for 20 chapters.

2. If the author has the physical and mental capacity to develop an argument. It is one thing to write the summary of a story and another thing is to write a telenovela.

3. The choice of the appropriate means of communication. Not always an argument can be developed for two different languages maintaining the same quality. Sometimes, more is lent for a television series than for a movie or vice versa.

In summary, when we write an argument, we must take into account all these factors since from them the project will be realized or not.

THE AUDIOVISUAL INDUSTRY:

The producer must be sensitive to those things that affect or influence the audience, that sensitivity and his knowledge of the audience will largely depend on his success or failure. Preferences or "ratings" may vary from one moment to another but are determined by the tastes of the audience and by the constant change of the story. It should also be determined in which markets the production will be placed, o at what times (if it is a television program) and in what screen (television channel). A cold analysis should be made of what are the costs and benefits of one or another schedule and one screen or another.

The next aspect, closely linked to trade is the management of budgets, hours of work and staff that are allocated to a project. Before beginning any project, however small it may be, a budget must be prepared based on the technical production script. Once the budget is finished, it must clearly show the costs of each line; technical equipment, personnel, transportation, food, lodging, makeup, scriptwriters, assistants, director of photography, audio technicians, lighting technicians, shooting special effects, specialized equipment for shooting such as cranes, rails, special lenses, steady cam, fabrics for chroma key, you must define how many days of the filming will be under study, in the City, in the interior of the country or abroad, if there are aerial shots, from a boat, or underwater, how many extras or models will participate in the filming, how many hours Pre-editing and post-production of video and audio requires the project, and how many hours dedicated to animations and special effects. When the budget has been completed you must add between 15 and 20% for unforeseen expenses.

A budget that is broken down has the advantage that, if it is necessary to cut it for lack of funds before starting the project, it can be clearly defined what item should be eliminated and how it will be replaced without affecting the quality of production.

ADVERTISING FINANCING

The "Product Placement" is a technique of financing and marketing that allows the producers of a film to solve some of the needs of production personnel through swaps, or sometimes for cash. You must shoot first and demonstrate the scene where the product or service of the sponsor is suggested and sign a document in which you agree to include it in the final version of the film to be released in theaters, or the television program. The product placement is not authorized until the scene in question has been shot. It can last a few seconds but the logos remain visible and also usually include short lines of dialogue depending on the contribution obtained.

Castings

When the production department is already defined, and has advanced several of the pre-production tasks is when it is ready for the calls of castings, which can be in several dates and strategic places, depending on the needs of the project.

Previously a very strict actress or actor profile was required for all the roles, nowadays it is not like that for secondary, incidental or extra roles.

o   • A sheet should be filled with information about each talent that appears at the casting,

o   • The session can be recorded on video camera,

o   • Costume tests can be done to personalize talent to what is sought,

o   • You should read fragments of the script

o   • And if they are long shifts, hours of food should be offered to the staff.

o   • The Acting coach or casting director intervenes in the final decision.

In the broad entertainment industry, a high standard of artistic and personal projection is also required, which combines many or almost all the frameworks of aesthetics and the expression of artistic concepts. For many this ideal of professional accomplishment entails many years of improvement in academies of diverse artistic expressions such as modeling, singing, acting, voice-overs, artistic direction of theater, radio, film and television, and even in the management of Public relations and beauty contests. Each artist has his own style, and that is why we always see in the midst of society movements or diverse artistic expressions that seek to highlight ideas, values, concepts and abstract metaphors that can be interpreted to be admired or rejected by a demanding and capitalist society; of which our opinion is also part.

Making the decision to become an artist means initiating a process of learning the right techniques to be able to mold the talent required to be considered by the coveted "talent takers", contest juries or investment partners. The degree of disappointment is high among the great majority of dreamers who swarm in the global society, with whom we can compete when launching or simply "try your luck", while perhaps we do not suppose either the great commitment of work, deprivation of society and risk involved in signing the various contracts that require compliance with a promotion agenda.

On the other hand, qualities are inherent and inherited. In the past it was considered that every son of an artist should be an artist too, or that baker's son should learn to make bread, the son of a blacksmith should grow by welding iron and so on. It is considered that the intelligence of a child is the ability to learn and understand and emphasizes the abilities and aptitudes to handle concrete situations, benefiting through the sensory experience.
Creating experimental conditions expose the potential that can be measured in quantitative terms that give it a level of qualification above its contemporaries, making it stand out for demonstrating its capabilities without much effort and naturally in the midst of its actions in the daily life.

We can not ensure that courses, independent studies, or class hours guarantee us success in our artistic career if we do not meticulously follow the steps to achieve it. The artistic possibilities are always influenced by physical limitations, which is what is called the social rank of artists. The social status of artists has been changing in the West over the centuries. In the classical age and in the Middle Ages, the poets and writers, using only intellectual capacity for their works, were considered creators of higher rank than the actors, dancers, musicians, painters and sculptors, who used manual or physical skill. But today the opposite occurs, where singers, actors and dancers are attracting a wider audience of consumers than poets, writers and painters as in other decades.

For better understanding, we will discuss them separately in order to list some recommendations as well as define their social functions.

• The voice: In the music industry, media and international entertainment, the voice management through voice over, singing, poetic declamation and voice dubbing are highlighted. It refers to the handling of the voice as melody   sung without accompaniment, with melodic rhythms and contours closely related to the rhythms of speech with the   relevant inflections of the text. The locution is more related to the field of broadcasting, both open and digital, television and the journalistic field and involves maintaining a medium tone of voice, with the help of sound amplification of the microphones, a fluent and correct language proficiency without the use of babbling and popular idioms. In recent years poetic recitals have made their way into cities, restaurants, parks and other cultural events with a renewed presence of poets representing the most varied literary trends. Finally, in relation to the use of the voice, we can mention that among the musical genres that have impacted the evolution of current cultural expressions are still the most popular African-American hip hop, electronics, pop, classic romantic ballads, reggae and the national folklore.

• The movement: Performing arts such as theater and dance in contemporary society, dances provide young people important occasions to meet, express conceptual figures of daily life and especially the rhythms or genres that arise in urban areas and suburban, to imply something without using words but with own style of dress. It is also feasible to work on experimental concepts aided by dance. The rhythmic movements are able to make work faster and more efficient, as in Japanese dances performed in rice plantations. In some cultures, such as the Latin, dance is a form of art, and in the twentieth century some dances that were originally religious rites or court entertainments have adapted to the theater. Thus, according to the classicist models, it differs from that of its contemporaries in a greater formal care in plots and verses. In his works the vices are always condemned, in the manner of a happy ending and exemplifying, against the pattern of the new comedies of the Spaniards Lope de Vega, Tirso de Molina, Guillén de Castro, Francisco Rojas Zorrilla, among others, who used to to draw exemplary consequences from situations where Christian values bordered the ambiguous and even dangerous limits. It is not until the mid-twentieth century that Latin American theater has acquired a certain personality, when dealing with its own subjects, taking as a starting point the reality of the spectator to whom it is destined.

Acting Coaching

A casting director or Acting Coach is someone who knows the script well. This document must also obtain the subjective level of the characters, as described by the scriptwriter based on the relationships between them and their personality.

THOUGHT + INTENTION = EMOTION

The work of the Acting Coach begins with the design of the casting, where a scene with its objective must be chosen, subsequently making the correct selection of the protagonist and co-protagonist cast.

The actor must handle 3 important aspects of his character:
· Memory
· Displacement or scenic movement.
· Own actor.

This advice begins in preproduction and is prior to filming. The actors must understand the point of view of the narrator, although the actor expresses himself through the characters whether it be preparation for film, television or theater. In these there are minor conflicts called "nuclei" and these are supposed to be emotional continuity that seeks to avoid overacting, in which some actors could drop unnecessarily adding text.

In writing there are two figures or two types of authors: the playwright or the screenwriter.

In audiovisual or cinematographic production for the interpretation of an argument two points of view are defined (p.v.):
- · P.V. of the screenwriter
- · P.V. from the director.

In this relationship, you must always specify any changes, substitution of characters' text, and report the authorized improvisations.

Each genre of film has a tone, no actor or actress should seem higher or lower, where the cast must live and have in mind the same movie.

The job of the Coach is to help discover things about the character that help to interpret it better, his story behind the conflicts, both in the frames and in the subplots of the film. Must ensure that pauses, turns and scene transitions are properly marked. Even veterans in this area of activity recommend that the director have knowledge of psychology.

POST CASTING PLAN

In this stage the casting director makes a meeting with all the actors of the cast of the film first of all to perform group dynamics that help to integrate the group, to test the chemistry between the actors forming mixed pairs. The most common are mouth exercises with corks, flavors and repetitions of the same dialogue with various moods such as angry, neutral and sad.

It continues with a group reading of the script, after which it is discussed on what to understand the character of each one. The coach will want to recognize what kind of actors he works with? How many weeks of rehearsal prior to filming will there be? Regularly work more with the protagonists since the secondary ones will have few scenes.

THE PRE-RUNNING:

If you have a camera, it is helpful to make them see themselves andso discuss with them interpretation corrections on stage. You should never impose a reasoning, you must respect to a certain extent the tricks, versatility and techniques of each actor and actress. Work according to the improvisation since the action can be changed.

The scenic interpretation must maintain a level of intimacy to build an inner world.

As for the use of closed plans, you should not abuse them to create privacy, but use it at the appropriate time, such as wink.

DURING THE FILMING:

Finally it is recommended to maintain synchrony all the staff: director, actors, assistants in the same direction.

The props or elements with which the actor must interact must be known in advance to the shooting. It is the director's job to indicate the scenic movement, evaluating and locating the expressive value in the place, example when the actors look at each other.

Shooting Plan

This is the document that will be prepared by the production manager, in order to eliminate some figures that increase the production budget. The summary omits information from the actors that will be mentioned in the call sheets.

SUMMARY OF THE RUNNING PLAN.

This document will take into account all the following:
- First page - The details of the production should be given. Title, phone number of all team members, as well as all those technically connected to the film.
- List of protagonists
- List of actors with the name of the characters they represent in the fiction and phone number.
- The trip - If necessary, information will be given of the trips, places of departure and the list of people who will make the trip. Information and schedule of means of transport if any person must go by their own means to the place of filming. Road maps for those who travel by car.

- Accommodations - If necessary, names, addresses and telephone numbers of the hotels where the team members will stay.
- Foreign and contacts - List of all locations, their addresses, telephone numbers and contact persons.
- Meeting place - The instructions for the time and place of meeting should be clear.
- Filming order - The order to be followed in filming is built on the basis of the required speed and availability of the actors and locations, making the best use of the time available.

In the case of Casting actors, letters will be used that will be noted in the names and days boxes for each specific task: T indicates work day, V indicates day of travel or transfer, and indicates a day of rehearsal. All three of these are paid. To indicate the start of the first and last day of work CE is used that indicates Beginning of Tests, and TF indicates day of Final Work. Finally, the periods of unemployment between working days are marked as D, which may indicate paid or not paid as you qualify.

For the action site will be contracted with a Field Producer or Road Manager, who will hire the necessary services for food, bath and others. For this, the directors will be given the filming plan with the information of the functions to be fulfilled day by day for the filming unit of recordings with actors. According to the scenes that are programmed for each recording day.

SHOOTING PLAN.
This is a complete compendium of all the details of each shooting day and it will be created by the director and his assistant director. The Filming Plan of the feature film will be made taking into account a set of issues:

- · Number of shooting days. The regular pattern is 30 - 40 days maximum.
- · Situation of the locations. It is better to shoot everything that corresponds to one location before moving to another, for reasons of time and organization.

- · Availability of recordings. If a location is only available on a certain date, the rest must adjust to this situation.
- · Availability of actors.

KEY IDEAS OF THIS CHAPTER

▶The Administration office is the fundamental center of all audiovisual projects, despite being of a temporary, from there the director, the producer, the assistants and other technical and artistic directors will take the decisions on how the total budget of the film will be used.

▶In the pre-production, vital documents appear for the success of the shoot. The department lists, translate into the cost of purchasing equipment that the project office should discard or assume in the manner that best suited for the costumes, props and supplies of the shooting period.

▶It is during pre-production that we must hire staff, establish schedules for artists and technicians, create documentation and reports necessary for an impeccable administration of the project that to let pass compromise transparency.

SUGGESTED ACTIVITIES

PERFORMANCE WORKSHOP:
1. Take dialogues and with your eyes covered add flavors to the palate of the actor.
2. Select actors and represent a scene in various moods.

MANAGEMENT WORKSHOP: Make the documentation of your project:
1. Choose a casting sheet format for actors.
2. Make the lists of each department with the necessary equipment for each scene on the page to page. Carry out the Filming Plan.
3. Make and deliver the call sheets for the shooting days according to actors on stage per day.

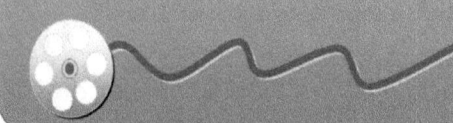

CHAPTER 7

PRODUCTION AND SHOOTING

- ▶ Field Producer
- ▶ Art Direction
- ▶ Lighting
- ▶ Photography
- ▶ Audio and sound
- ▶ Pre Edition and Data Managing
- ▶ Electricity

- ▶ The Director
- ▶ First Assistant
- ▶ Second assistant
- ▶ Continuity
- ▶ Steering Theory

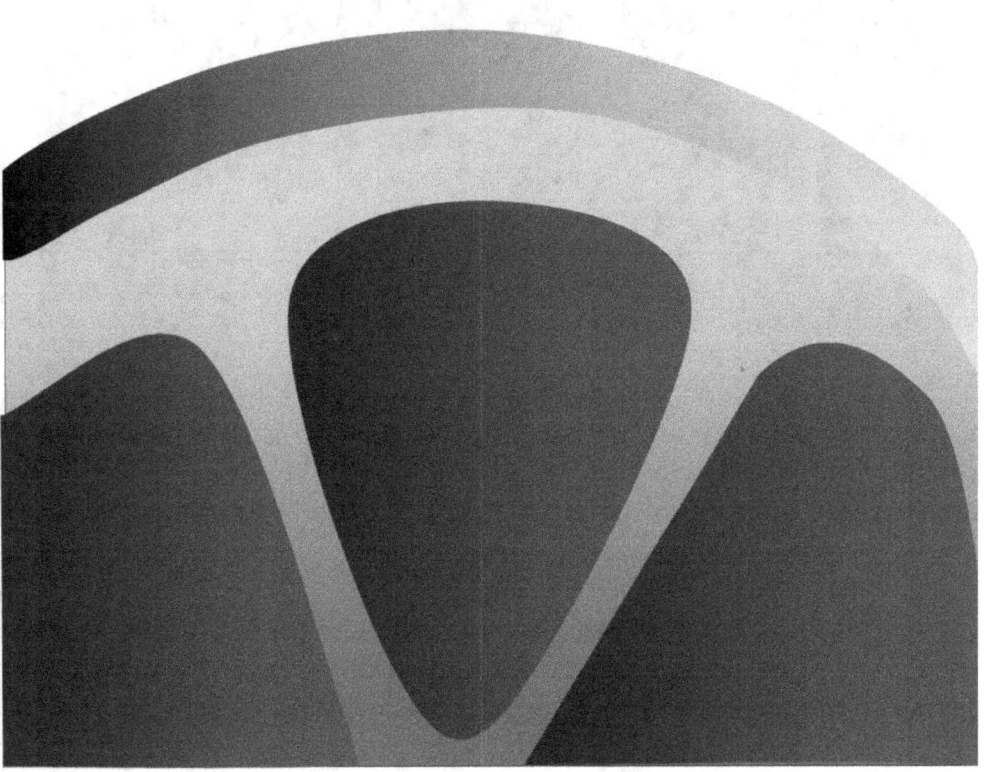

Production & Shooting

The first day of shooting a film is a unique and enriching experience. A large number of people. They work in unison to achieve the magic of creating a time and space that emerged from the imagination of the writers. This time lapse which can be minutes or hours is able to entertain, entertain and excite millions of viewers through the screens. The entertainment industry goes ahead, suffering losses, finding sudden successes and improving in quality as never before seen. Here we will know who is behind.

Film production, includes the set of specialists involved in making a film. The cinema is an art and an industry. It is also a means of communication of great influence in society. The description that is detailed below refers to the areas that are made in fiction feature films and with professional actors.

The main goal of the shoot is to obtain the shots without errors of each scene of our script. Previously the development of 35 mm was used but since the appearance of the panoramic camera, digital cinema and hard disks of large terabytes of capacity, the previous model changed to make way for the era of high definition and image resolution.

The director is the absolute responsible for the creative aspect, and the producer, the financial from the development. Other roles of responsibility are played by the continuist, the data manager, the production manager, the assistant director, the director of photography, the image and sound editors, the music composer and the costume designers (costume designer) and the scenography or artistic director.

Field Producer

The field producer is an important figure during the beginning of the shooting since in the location he is in charge of representing the producer in the action site.

It is the person who coordinates and demands that all technical needs be met, such as: food or catering service, accommodation for foreign actors, equipment and car safety, and required transportation.

This field producer should have at his hands such important documents as a copy of:

- Permits for use of lease by public authorities.
- Support personnel such as ambulance, firemen and police if the scene is shot in areas that involve certain risks such as red zones, beaches, use of fire, etc.
- It is customary to use car rental service, airlines, water bottles that can even be exchanged for Product Placement after negotiation with the companies.

It should be considered that people who share a room are compatible since sometimes there are differences or enmities and should be noted in writing the amenities to which the guest or talent will be entitled to avoid charges.

Art Direction

The Art Direction is a term that is born from the staging, which in the theater means to put on a show on stage. And its main objective is to describe the shape and composition of the elements that appear in the camera frame. It includes the design, creation and arrangement of all the elements visible in the film, such as books, glasses, drunk drinks and why. The art director is a set designer, a costume designer, a make-up artist, a cast supervisor and an interior decorator; all that at the same time.

The production design carried out by an art director takes into account the following factors:

- · There are directors who know what they want for the decoration of their film and others ask for an art proposal. In general, he is not hired on a payroll, but is offered for professional services.
- · Space, colors, objects and forms must be taken into account for any art proposal.
- · Bear in mind that the elements to be budgeted will have real functionality, they can not be unnecessary.
- · You must know the location in advance. There are things that are removed from the original place to make room for new ideas.
- · Must know about current, past and old-fashioned fashions.
- · If it is a single change of costumes for talent, you must have double costumes.

In addition to the aspects shared with the theatrical show, the filmic staging includes:

- aspects of cinematography.
- Camera movements

- scale
- sizes of the planes
- Lighting
- decorated
- locker room
- makeup
- cast
- direction and movement of the actors

In turn, these components represent the following factors of the scene that the staging encompasses:
- Elements of global production design
- Built or natural scenery
- Elements of human component
- Direction and distribution of the actors in the frame
- Constitution of a specific time and space.
- The plan of the decoration has to faithfully follow the plan of the action.
- Its decoration must not only be illuminable, rodable, photographed, but it must also be true.
- That has character, that character that makes a street in Bilbao does not look like a street on the Italian border.

THE HARMONY OF COLOR

The perception of color is considered a physical phenomenon of light or vision, associated with the different wavelengths in the visible area of the electromagnetic spectrum. As a sensation experienced by humans and certain animals, the perception of color is a very complex neurophysiological process. The methods currently used for the specification of color fall into the specialty called colorimetry, and consist of precise scientific measurements based on the wavelengths of three primary colors.

An art director must know the classification of colors:
- · Analogous colors
- · The monochromatic colors

- · Complementary

Another tool is the color palette, which is chosen together with the director of the program or film or with the director of photography to define the artistic vision of the story and cooperate with its narrative. Classic examples of color association with the character are "The Wizard of Oz", "The Godfather" that introduced the leitmotive or singular sound.

The scenography or decoration fulfills an expressive and significant function in the cinema, such as the following:
- · Simulation of reality. Example: a small village in the West in the last century.
- · It must be functional, not static.
- · Symbolic of certain lines of psychological annotation as in German Expressionism or in film noir.

The scenario can be natural or artificial, and project to the audience:
- · Extreme verisimilitude, reality effect.
- · Pretend through transparencies
- · To assume them as such explicit decorations.

Each of the ways play a dramatic or narrative role. They can by themselves be carriers of a specific semantic function. For example: Cactus that replaces the rose that has never seen the protagonist in "The man who killed Liberty Valance" John Ford, 1962.

It must be illuminated. The objective that sees the set is not the eye that sees life. A room in which one lives is not a room in which one rolls. The decoration is based on the script, it is not an end in itself.

ART IN PRE-PRODUCTION STAGE

The page by page is reduced to a checklist. From the first reading of the script it can be that the production design is intuitive, without annotations. This is achieved by seeking a sensory contact with the story and its visual references.

If there is something that is not understood in the interpretation, communication should be maintained with the director. Another valuable recommendation is to follow the rule of the questions: who ?, what ?, when ?, where? and because? The character belongs to an era, or environment that denotes what the theme of the story is. In a second reading of the script the visual references of the script are collected.

The original colors are proposed in the budget, which includes decoration, ambience and concept. We work by lists of each element such as: all the props, all the costumes, all the hairstyles, etc. Avoid bad combinations of textures with textures, bright colors with opaque or dark, etc.

MOOD BOARDS

They are similar to the well-known "collage". A collage is a pictorial technique that consists of pasting various materials such as canvas, wood, paper or cardboard on a flat surface.

The decisive and characteristic difference between collage technique (from the French coller, paste) and painting is that instead of creating an image with color and line, the drawing is constructed with apparently incompatible materials such as newspapers, photographs, illustrations, fabrics , wood, feathers and wire, actually with anything that can be attached to a surface. Applied objects can be combined with painted fragments.

In the creation of Mood Boards it is not necessary to be so detailed, if it is useful to make them to express to the project managers how the plot makes you feel.

Sketching and scale: They are also made per character. Example: Black Swan.

Finally, in the following meetings with the director, you should:

- · Unify points of view.
- · Visual references should be carried out: photos, collages, mood boards, etc.
- · You should avoid imposing personal taste, for example listening to music that you do not like.
- · The transfer of the furniture or objects must be arranged with the production assistant, the times or schedules must be foreseen, and have the approval of the director, regarding the budget and billing already squared.

Lighting

All shooting in video or digital cinema requires lighting to obtain the best image quality, without shadows on the lens or face, without loss of data, and without undesired end effects on the screen. The bulb, also called lamp or bulb, is a vacuum-made glass structure that carries inside it a filament made of a very high melting point material, which becomes incandescent to the passage of the electric current, thus producing the light.

The material with which the filament is manufactured must have a very high melting point because it is necessary to increase the temperature a lot so that the ratio between the light energy and the thermal energy generated by the filament is profitable. The first bulbs used carbon filaments, but nowadays they are made with extremely fine tungsten or tungsten wires, whose melting temperature is 3,410 ° C. The thread is so fine that the displacement of the electrical charges through it makes it reach temperatures above 2,500 ° C.

According to its characteristics, the focus can be halogen, tungsten or fluorescent.

- · Halogen: Most modern lamps are of this type. They are yellow lights that generate great temperature, that is, they are redder. Its name is due to the fact that this type of spotlights are filled with a small quantity of halogen gases such as nitrogen and krypton.

- · Tungsten: They are foci whose filament inside the glass structure, is made of a metal of gray color, very hard and difficult to fuse with other elements. They are less common in the audiovisual field than the other types. Its disadvantage is that it generates a lot of heat so it requires air conditioning and the focus of this type is short-lived.

- · Fluorescent: The fluorescent lamp is another type of electric discharge device with general lighting applications. It is a low pressure mercury vapor lamp contained in a glass tube, coated in its interior with a fluorescent material such as phosphorus.

In science, the scale most used is the absolute scale or Kelvin, invented by the British mathematician and physicist William Thomson, Lord Kelvin. In this scale, the absolute zero, which is located at -273.15 ° C, corresponds to K, and a difference of one kelvin equals a difference of one degree in the centigrade scale. In audiovisual production it is a fictitious measure to know the amount of luminosity of the real color in the environment. It is an abstract concept that expresses the color of light and relates temperature to light. It is measured in Kelvin. The higher the temperature in degrees K, the blue will be the light we are working with, and as soon as it has less temperature it will be more red.

ILLUMINATION	
EXTERIOR	INTERIOR
5,600 ° k.	3,200 ° k.
(Daylight)	(Artificial light)

Artificial light gives a light temperature of about 3,200 ° K, and daylight gives a light temperature of about 5,600 ° K.

Additionally there are some additives that are added to the lights, and others that are used outdoors such as filters and bounces.

Filters:

Filters are reinforced plastic films that come in several colors, but the three main ones are: red, yellow and blue. The use of filters form an important part in the aesthetic proposal of all films, both indoors and outdoors. Highly successful films that refer to feelings of sadness, hate or helplessness use blue or cold. The warm ones like the yellow or orange filter represent action, heat and dynamism. Dark filters such as black promote fear, which is not to say it textually but to represent it figuratively.

The Scottish mechanical engineer is the one who incorporates the feedback principle of a servomechanism, by articulating the output circuit with the input circuit, which is the basic concept of automation. The watt electric unit was named after him. He was also a famous civil engineer, who did several studies on canal tracks.

APPROXIMATE CONVERSION OF TEMPERATURE OF THE LIGHT	
KELVIN	WATT
2700	1 lamp up to 60
3,500	1 lamp up to 13
5,500	2 fluorescent lamps up to 13

Bouncers:

Pure white structures are called rebounders or softeners used outdoors in the direction of sunlight as a natural resource during filming. The different sources of light remove the shadows and level the intensities from different positions.

The person in charge of lighting in a location must know what fillings and main lights will be used to create the visual atmosphere requested by the director of the production to be shot at any time of the day. All the lighting that is placed in front of the camera has to meet a precise objective. In general, the lighting depends both on the previous conditions of luminosity and darkness, as well as atmospheric conditions, especially when it comes to exteriors and artificial lighting that is available in the place.

CHARACTERISTICS OF THE LIGHT

1. Intensity: It is the brightness of the light that affects the exposure.
2. Quality: If the shadow is soft, it should be nuanced or even annulled. And if it is darkness it is more dense it will produce harsh shadows, which also have a dramatic utility.
3. Contrast: It is the ratio or ratio between the brightness of the most illuminated and darkest areas.
4. Temperature of the colors: intensity that affects the quality of the artistic composition.

THE INTENSITY OF LIGHT

Professional photographers and demanding amateurs use photometers and exposure meters to measure the intensity of light in a given situation and thus determine the proper combination of velocity and diaphragm aperture. Four types of photometers are basically used: incident light, reflected light, spot and flash, although, properly speaking, spot photometers are a type of the reflected light and flash photometers can be both incident and reflected.

Three basic rules of natural lighting are the following:
1. There will not be enough intrusion of light into the camera if the light or shadow on the lens is too poor.
2. If the opening of the iris or diaphragm is too closed.
3. If a very dense filter is used with respect to the tones or brightness of the frame.

They also produce contrast and create volume in the subject. All white surfaces introduced into the panorama where colors predominate tend to alter the measurement of light.

ELEMENTS OF EXTERIOR OR HARD ILLUMINATION

Because the sun is far away from us, it is considered a point source of light. Its rays illuminate us in a straight line and produce harsh shadows.

The advantages of hard light are:
- · Directionality that restricts and profiles.
- · The shadow produced which in turn clearly shows the textures.

The disadvantages of this type of light are:
- · The generation of certain inevitable shadows.
- · The result may seem harsh, contrasted and unattractive.
- · The limited dispersion that requires the use of many directed light bulbs with the consequent appearance of multiple strong shadows.

ELEMENTS OF INTERIOR OR SOFT LIGHTING

Within a study with few or no natural light windows, several sources of artificial light should be used, ie diffuse light lamps, which scatter in all directions.

One of the forms of diffuse light is that which the sun emits when it is hidden behind a cloud that reflects its light on rough and clear surfaces.

The shadows tend to fade and there are slight variations in the brightness of the surfaces so that they and their surroundings are very inaccurate in the image.

There are several ways to provide soft light:
1. The first is based on diffusion materials such as glass sheets, grinding or paper that is placed on the light source to reduce its intensity and soften its quality.
2. Another way is the maneuvers of incidence of rebound of the light on a parabolic reflector achieving the appearance of lights on the shadows of the object.

The advantage of using soft light are:
- · That can produce subtle or delicate shadows.
- · Does not create unwanted shadows
- · It can illuminate shadows produced by hard lighting so that the details can be seen without producing more shadows.
- · The soft light source can cover a large part of the scene.

Its disadvantages are the following:
- · Illuminates all kinds of textures and shapes of the surface.
- · It is completely dispersed that fills the whole image with light and makes it very difficult to restrict it to a certain area.
- · The intensity that decreases rapidly with distance and forces the lamps closer to the scene.

CHARACTERISTICS OF ARTIFICIAL LIGHT

The Contrast: Consists of the difference of light between the lightest and darkest areas of the image. It depends on the tones or complexion of the subjects, the variations of the luminous intensity and the projected shadows.

Direction of the light: It can influence considerably the impression produced by any object used. The director of lighting or "lighting director" can demonstrate it by standing in front of a mirror in a dark room and arranging or lighting a spotlight and you can see how the effects vary as the position of the point of light changes.

Photographic triangle: This lighting system is designed for the realization of an image in dark clear or Rembrant style. It is used in three basic directions where the following results are obtained:

- o King light or main light that should be located slightly above and to the side of the camera. Usually it is a strong light in kelvin or watt, which delineates the forms and surfaces of the subjects.

- o Filling light or fill light: This lamp is located on the opposite side of the camera to illuminate the shadows and reduce contrasts. As the main light is more cocked, the fill light will be more important. It has two parts the spoot that it directs, and the floot that it fills.

- o Back light or hair light: which is placed behind, kicker area that points down on the subject and will provide solidity to the background. The kicker also called effect or separation light by its position with respect to the camera must be barely perceptible to the eye.

PHOTOGRAPHIC TRIANGLE

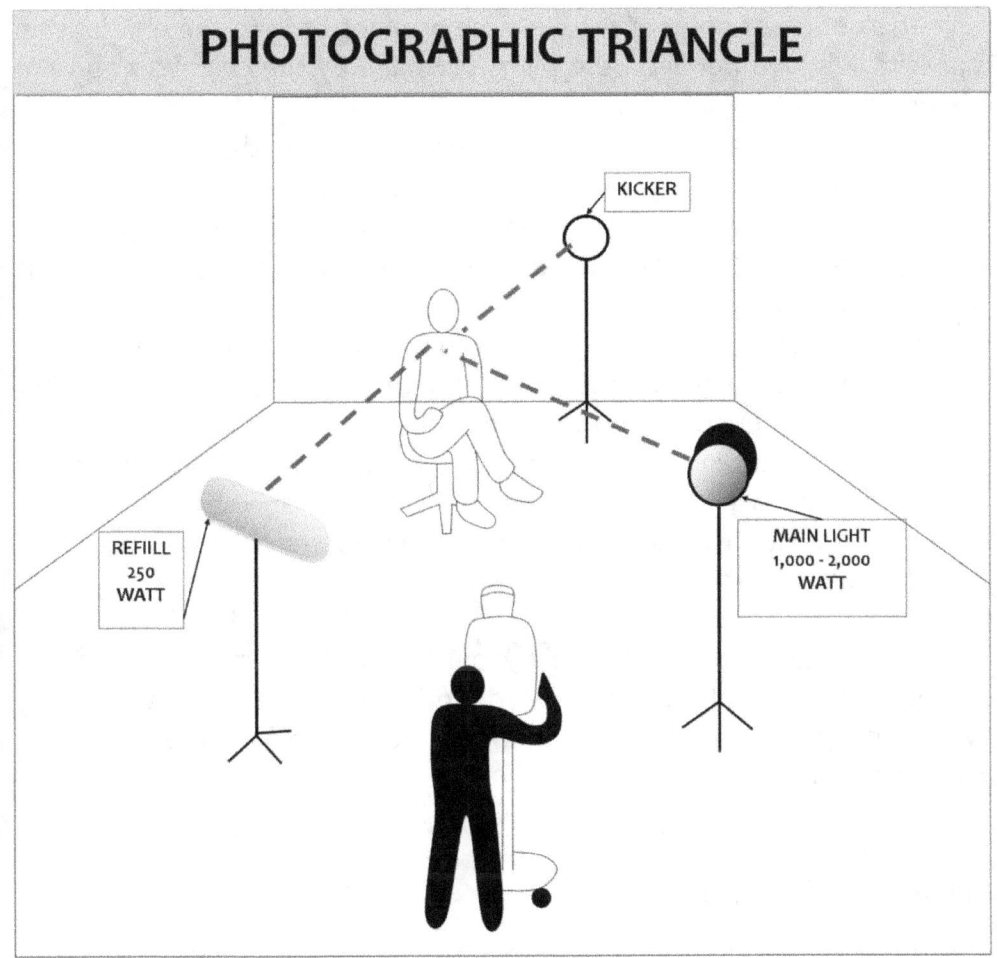

Photography

The director of photography, also known as the operator, or first operator (facing the camera, which would be the second), works closely with the director and interprets in terms of lighting the director's needs in terms of the atmosphere and atmosphere of each shot . Other operators can intervene in the production to shoot special effects or camera tricks that help to give dimension and meaning of the show to a movie.

The notion of point of view is here brought back to the relationship that is maintained between the place occupied by the character and the one occupied by the camera.

- • Ocularization: Relationship between what the camera shows and what the character is supposed to see.
- • Ocularization zero: cases in which the place occupied by the camera does not identify with the occupied by any diegetic instance.
- • Secondary internal ocularization: when the subjectivity of an image is constructed through montage, raccords or any other procedure of contextualization.
- • Primary internal ocularization: in cases where a mark on the image allows it to be identified as a place of a character absent from it ("the moved ones," which characterize this or that plane as "subjective").

The situation that the film sound is not lateralized (with the exception of stereophony), or located a priori in a visual source, and may even come from outside the world of the diegesis, makes the analysis of auricularization quite complex.

OPERATION OF THE VIDEO CAMERA

The photochemical effect of light is the principle used for the formation of the image in the video camera.

The video camera consists of several elements that are involved in the formation, processing and sending of the image, these elements are:

a) The lens picks up the image of the object and sends it to the prism.

b) The prism decomposes the light reflected by the objects or people in three colors: red, blue and green and sends them in turn to the electronic cannons or "image analysis tubes"

c) Electronic cannons (also called image analysis tubes or iconscopes) these cannons collect the electronic beams of the three basic colors (blue, green and red) each canon explores the basic color that corresponds to it and sends it to a screen called "Photoemitting Mosaic or Photoconductive Plate" that is explored by a beam of electrons which impinge on the mosaic through a magnetic field, sweeping the screen in a determined way beginning with the odd numbers; 1, 3, 5, 7, 9. .. until you reach the bottom of the screen and conclude the odd series run, then jump to even numbers, 2, 4, 6, 8 ... until you complete 525 lines per frame (frame). phase of a movement captured by the television camera in 1/30 of a second in the NTSC system (National Television System Comitee) The horizontal route is performed 15,750 times, each time a cycle is completed, whether odd or even a field is formed. Two Fields complete a frame _ Each time a cycle is completed, whether odd or even, a Field is formed.

d) Pre-amplifiers collect the signal from the electronic cannons, process it and amplify it by sending it to the amplifiers.

e) The amplifiers amplify the signal and send it to the processors.

f) Processors insert the synchronism so that the signal gives more pulses and is synchronous in the monitor.

The new techniques have been displacing the image tubes (iconoscopes) in conventional video cameras and today it is the sensors of the solid state image that perform the function of the old image tube. These solid state image sensors are much cheaper, lighter, consume less energy and capture the image with higher resolution in extreme low light conditions, plus they can capture direct light from any light source (including the sun) without any damage to the operation of the camera.

BASIC TECHNIQUES OF MULTIMEDIA PHOTOGRAPHY

The success of Field Production depends, most of the time, on the organization of the filming. The process of pre-production that includes the search of locations, talent, props, construction of scenographies, organization and fluidity of the filming is crucial for the efficient development of production. A good producer is first and foremost an organizer in all aspects related to production, both in time and in human resources and budget financed.

Producing videos, films, documentaries or fiction is closely linked to three aspects that the Producer / Director must manage: television and cinema are an industry that unites commerce, technique and art. The proper management of these three aspects require knowledge from the director in the three branches.

EIGHT BASIC PRINCIPLES OF CONFORTABLE EDITION

GENERALITIES
The edition is the process by which the pictures of a film are united, giving it logic and continuity. It is a process of composition where each picture must be linked to another until it forms an "all". This union of pictures is also a sum of times that creates the UNITY.

The cinematographic and video image consists of five basic factors: 1. Light, 2. Color, 3. Plane, 4. Composition, 5. Filming angle.

These factors are essential to unite the tables.
Understanding comfortable editing the "juxtaposition" of the different pictures that make up the film or video, so that it is pleasant to the process of visual, logical and coherent reception and does not force the public's conscience.

The actions that take place on the screen must have the same logic as they do in reality.

As we will now refer to the juxtaposition of the tables, it is convenient to indicate the table definitions and their characteristics:

• PICTURE: The process of filming and fixing the film, videotape or optical disc of a given object or subject, group of things or people is called a picture; from the ignition to the shutdown of the camera.

• TABLE COMPOSITION: It is the name given to the parts that make up the image and that have as an essential characteristic the dynamism, its interaction, the relationship with the background and dramaturgical content.
• PHOTOGRAM TABLE: It is the phase of a movement captured by the camera. In 35mm cinema it corresponds to 1/24 of a second, in video of the NTSC system 1/30 of a second.

The most used format of the professional film that is the 35mm for every second there are 24 frames. In the NTSC video system in every second there are 30 frames.

I PRINCIPLE - EDITING BY APPROACH

Editing is a process that must be foreseen when writing a technical script and drawing the story board, but for this a certain training of the imagination is required to feel the effect of the change of the pictures on the screen. This training begins with the location of the camera in relation to the subject; what portion of the subject will be fixed by the camera and how that portion will look on the screen.

The change from one approach to another must be sufficiently noticeable but not abrupt, so that the public does not lose the orientation and the sensation of the actions that take place. The public should not be forced to force their conscience to understand what is happening in front of their eyes.

Practice has shown that the union of two tables is easily accepted when the difference between them is sufficient but not noticeable. The transition from a close plane to another more open close plane is accepted by visual reception with fluency.

You should not edit a close plane with a general one without having between them a medium plane of the subject.

The order and steps of an edition that complies with the principle of approach is as follows:

Very general plan ↔ General plan ↔ Mid-American plan ↔ Medium plan open ↔ Closed plan ↔ Open plan close ↔

Closed plan close ↔ Detail plan.

This order responds to the comfortable condition of editing by approach. If you shoot a rocket, an elephant, an ant or a building, for all these cases the principle will be the same.

This principle loses its strength when you want to make an accent anywhere in the development of the action or when a change is made from one painting to another subject that according to the plot is at a great distance.

II. PRINCIPLE - EDITING ACCORDING TO THE ORIENTATION IN THE SPACE

This principle is applied in many cases when you want to establish a relationship between subjects who have been filmed separately and must see each other. The main task is how to locate the camera so that it produces the visual impression that events take place as if they were seen in real life. This filming requires the organization of the space and the camera must be placed on one side of the line of the gaze of the characters, this construction of the space on the screen clarifies the action that takes place between the characters.

This rule has equal validity for the correlation of different objects; a painter and his canvas, a tank and a cannon that shoots him. If it is decided at the time of filming to cross the line of correlation between subjects and change their orientation in space, this must occur before the eyes of the public through a panorama or a dolly panorama (traveling) or with a change of angle of filming through a front point of one of the subjects.

When more than two people participate in a conversation, it becomes more complicated to maintain spatial orientation during the filming process. The filming should start with a reference to a general map of the three people and then keep the filming area on one side of the eye.

In diagram 2b point 4 is incorrect since the subject "C" can not be joined with another frame because it changes the direction of his gaze. Filming can be done from any area except those that are marked on the diagram. Mastery of this aspect of the edition is essential for the chronicle, since there is no time to prove the security of the edition. If it is a congress and in the gallery there is a speaker and the room is completely full of people, the orientation should be based on the direction of the gaze of the members of the main table and choosing one of the sides of the direction of the meeting. their looks.

In the diagram of the members of the main table Come from right to left and the public from left to right. (camera point 3) If it is a meeting you must keep one side of the eyes.

III. PRINCIPLE - EDITING ACCORDING TO THE DIRECTION OF AN OBJECT IN MOTION IN THE BOX

This principle is related to all objects that move on the screen. Any change of trajectory of the object or subject is better demonstrated in one of the frames, the end and the beginning of the frames must correspond. If, for example, a cavalry moves from left to right and in the next frame it moves from right to left, the visual reception will have the impression that they are being returned and the public may think that they were frightened and flee, but if It shows why this change of direction, a curve in the road, a hill, a turn in the street, the change of direction will be clear.

If for example, a vehicle moves from the camera to the bottom a little to the left and in the next frame the same vehicle moves from the camera to the bottom, a little to the right; these boxes can not be edited.

Any sudden change of direction of a moving object is better demonstrated on the screen, for this it is necessary to shoot a transition box where the change of direction is shown.

To deepen the essence of this principle, we will use conditional images. The movement of the vehicle on the screen can be fixed on the story board with vectors. The movement can be carried out in four directions and the vectors go from the center.

This is the schematic expression of the image in four frames of a vehicle in motion for a comfortable visual reception of a change of direction that is expressed graphically and must not exceed the angle of 90 degrees.

IV PRINCIPLE - EDITION ACCORDING TO THE PHASE OF THE OBJECTS THAT MOVE IN THE BOX

This principle is related to objects that perform movements by phases, for example: a marine wheel or a carousel.

Let's suppose that we are going to film a barge and that the box in which our character is going is blue, start shooting with a very general shot of the marine wheel when it starts to move slowly and the box of our character begins to ascend. first in the lower left part of the box and then in the upper part until reaching the maximum height point and then it starts to descend. The descent we want to film it with a general plan of the box where our character goes. For this box to respond to a comfortable condition by "phase" we must start filming before the box enters the box, continue it when it is in the box and conclude when it has left the box.

People also fulfill phases in their movements, for example: if we have a character that rises from a chair in a general plane and want to move to a lateral plane of the same character rising from the chair, the interpreter must perform the full phase and with all the details both in the general plane and in the lateral midplane so that in both tables the phase is fulfilled and they can be joined.

If we shoot the steps of a person who is playing from left to right of the screen, in the middle lateral plane and then we want to film in the frontal general plane we must take into account all the details of the walk and the foot with which he took "that last step to make the change "of plane and begin to film from the repetition of" that last step "and the foot with which it was made.

V PRINCIPLE - EDITION ACCORDING TO THE TEMPO OF MOVING OBJECTS

The union of two frames that reflect the movement of an object or subject must correspond to an adequate tempo from frame to frame. The sudden change of tempo from one frame to another can "mean and only mean" a change in the course of events on the screen.

In cases where the tempo must accelerate from one frame to another, it must be done through a progress of the development of the internal action of the plane. If a young girl runs through the streets of a city at the same speed; the mathematical significance of the frequency of its steps, where each second must be of the same duration and with the same frequency change the steps.

If we want to make a change in the tempo of the steps of an actor that runs moving from right to left of the screen and in frame 1 moves 4 steps / seconds, in frame 2 moves 4 steps / seconds and in the frame 3 moves to 2 steps /

Second; It will give the impression that the subject is going to stop. 1 = 5 Steps / sec 2 = 5 Steps / sec 3 = 4 Steps / sec 4 = 4 Steps / sec 5 = 3 Steps / sec

When the object that moves in the frame does not perform cyclic movements, such as a car or a boat, the expression of the tempo will be the speed with which the movement is made in relation to the background and frame of the frame.

There are two variants in which the difference in the tempo of the movement of the object can be revealed.

a) When the two paintings are aesthetically filmed and the speed of the moving object is revealed in relation to the frame of the painting.

b) When the two frames are filmed with the apparatus moving from a fixed point, a panorama following the object that moves.

In the second case, the coordinate system for measuring the velocity will be the background on which the object is mounted in the frame.

The time it takes for the car to pass through frame No. 1 of diagram 5d will be approximately three seconds, while the time it will take the car to pass through square No. 2 will be only 1 second. For the public the distance between the left frame of the frame and the right frame is the same, but the time for the execution of that time, conditionally equal in its distance will be reduced three times and the public will have the feeling that the car in the second picture moves three times faster and that does not happen in real life. To increase the speed of a car, an acceleration time is necessary. If we join tables 1 and 2 of the diagram as a result of that union, we will obtain an unreal situation.

To carry out two conditions of comfortable editing by approach and by tempo, it is necessary that the distance traveled by the car is equal in both frames and at the same speed.

The change from square "a" to square "b" will be fluid.

When two frames are filmed through a panorama, for the audience a possible violation of the tempo unit of the movement can occur if the subject of attention is at a much smaller distance from the camera in relation to the previous one and the background. the same.

To join two scenarios one should try to consider three basic points:
1. The Plane

2. Speed of the moving object

3. Distance between the object and the background

If we are going to join a square "a" with a square "b" and the square "a" was filmed with an open half-plane view of a moving Sailboat, the "b" plane must be filmed with another "a" panorama the same speed of frame "a" and with a medium plane more open or closed. This same rule applies to static objects.

VI PRINCIPLE - EDITION BY COMPOSITION ACCORDING TO THE CENTER OF ATTENTION IN THE BOX

The center of attention of the screen is 80% to the left or right of the screen. That point of attention must be conserved so that people or objects do not jump from one side to another at the moment of joining the pictures.

The figures we see in diagram 6 can be edited by approach, by orientation in space, but not by composition because in the first frame the subject appears on the left and in the second frame appears on the right. The vision has fixed with all its sharpness the position of the character in the left part of the screen, but in the consequent picture the character has disappeared and the public is required an effort to find it, while the public looks for the character a part of the action will have been lost, the reception process has been violated and the message of the painting will have disappeared.

The same happens in two people who speak and one is on his back and the other in front of the camera, if the movement of the characters from one side of the picture to another is not recorded by the camera, the position of the subjects must be preserved. objects in the box

VII PRINCIPLE - LIGHTING EDITION

The principle of editing by illumination includes the calculation of the change of illumination, the character of the background and the luminous character of one painting to another.

In diagram 7a the character is on a dark background in diagram 7b the character is on a background illuminated by the beam of light that penetrates the window. To make a change from a background with low lighting to an illuminated background while preserving the fluidity of the paintings, it is necessary in the paintings to link a detail o the background; a painting, a vase, a window, a detail of the wall, etc. (see diagram 7c).

In practice it happens with certain frequency that in a general plane the personage had the right part of his body illuminated, and in a half plane the left part. Probably something could bother the filming process with the consequent result that those pictures "will not be able to join".

For such situations of "breakdown" that arise in the editing process, it must be remembered that the change in background lighting must not exceed 1/3 of the surface of the frame. The shadow of the actors' nose may be a bit longer or shorter but it should not jump from right to left or from left to right. When we illuminate in nature we must take into account that the direction of the sun's rays changes position as the day goes by, we should not initiate an illumination of a location with sun and end with a dark day.

VIII PRINCIPLE - EDITION ACCORDING TO THE LOCATION OF THE FILMING AXIS

The imaginary line formed between a subject and the camera in front of it is called "axis" (Diagram 8a). If you want to make a change from a general plane to a medium one and then to a close one, keeping the same axis and the same direction, you will have the feeling that the subject "jumps" towards the camera, to avoid that jump in the change of planes you must move the camera to the character and two steps to the left or right of the previous axis, this process will result in a slight change in the composition of the picture that the public will accept easily. That change of composition will facilitate a measure of necessary contrast between two neighboring frames for a comfortable reception.

THE FILLING BOX

The "filling" box is the picture of one or more details of the locations, characters, objects and parallel events that can serve as "relief for the filling between two tables that can not be edited for violation of any of the principles, "We must not lose sight that the filling box should go according to the character of the film and bring associations related to the subject we present, it should not be a dead entity located out of context, this is the essence of the filling box, a edit value and a dramatic content value.

STANDARD SHOOTS IN PHOTOGRAPHY

Both in cinematography and in the television industry, a shot or shot is the smallest element of recorded or filmed material. A set of related planes make up a scene, and the scene is a unit that contains continuous dramatic action, in a succession of shots by time, space, event, theme, concept, motivation or character. A scene is a series of related shots, but also a single scene can be a single shot.

The sequence is a longer segment, made up of a series of closely related scenes. In the sequences the events happen in continuous form associated with each other, they can also happen at different times and places, but they are related to the main story and they give coherence and follow-up to it.

When the objective of the camera is a person or a group, the following plans are used:
- · Closed Plane: Known in its acronym in English as Close Up, is the taking of the shoulders to the top of the head.

This is widely used in novels, interviews, beauty programs, etc.
- · Big Close up: Take closed to the face of the model or talent.

- · Extreme closed plane: Completely closed shot to a detail of the face. It is also known Extreme Close Up (ECU).
- · Medium Closed Plane: Take half of the thorax to the top of the head.
- · Medium shot: Known in English as Medium shot (MS) is a shot taken from the waist to the top of the head. Used mainly in newscasts.
- · Medium Two shot: Known as (MTS), it is the shot that is made to two talents from the waist to the top of the head.
- · Reference plane or Two Shot: (TS) Two-talents full body shot. If there were three talents, the shot is called Three Shot, however there is no shot called Four Shot or similar. Within a group of three or more talents or actors, the reference plane is used, which includes two people who converse within the group, avoiding showing the others.
- · Medium long shot: Take from the knees to the top of the head. It is also known as an American plane.
- · Long shot: Also known as Long Shot, Full Shot or Body shot, it is a shot of the whole body of talent, where the important thing is the body of the model and not the scenery.

When the objective of the camera is an external location or set design, the following plans are used:

- · Open Plane: It is a shot where the landscape and talent are important, but the camera does not move as it does in the panorama.
- · Panoramic or Wide Shot: In this shot does not matter the figure of talent, but the scenography or landscape around it. By offering all the elements in the scene, it provides an orientation to the viewer. It is divided into Paninng horizontal or paninng which is a movement from side to side or right to left or vice versa. And the movement of the crane where the cameraman moves from a crouched position to standing, suggests sensuality, superiority and surprise.

- · Product shot: It is a closed shot of a product, which is usually done by advertising it by means of a prior signature of a guideline through a television station or production company.
- · Tight Shot: Take a detail of a product or object closed.
- · Complementary Action Plan: Taking support that in edition is associated with the action within the location previously shown, but not identical. It is mainly used to show a person who approaches the main talent. It is also known as Cut-away.
- · Aberrant plane: Motion shot in an oblique direction to the frame, it is never vertical or completely horizontal, since it is done with the help of a crane or rails.
- · Subjective Planes: They are a set of three sub subjective categories: the plane at the level of the view; shows the actor or talent looking towards the camera, giving the impression that he is talking to us. In action the subjective planes are those where reality is manipulated and performed as a sequence, for example when we see a girl who takes a book and reads it is the objective plane; here the subjective sequence is a detailed plan of the content of the book, from a shoulder angle of the girl.

CAMERA MOVEMENTS AND ANGLES

- · Panning or Panning: It is a horizontal movement from right to left or vice versa, on the axis of the camera. Imitate the movement of our head when we look at the horizon. Panning is essential to cover action sequences. It can also be used to show very long objects that need to be seen in a single shot without cuts. The panning is done with a tripod or with the camera over the shoulder. The tripod ensures a smoother movement to the shot. As a rule you should pan slowly, and leave approximately 5 seconds for any object to move from one side of the frame to the other; which will give the viewer enough time to absorb the details. On the other hand, there should not be panning of reverse or to record in half.

- · Picado or Tilt Up: It is a camera movement that could be translated as pitch. Imitate the movement of the head when we look from the bottom up or vice versa. It is basically a vertical panning and is used to follow an object that moves in this direction. Like the horizontal pan, it should be started with a static shot and at the end to give the viewer enough time to register the subject. When it is from the bottom up, it is called Picado or Tilt Up, which is composed of scenes from low angles lying down on the floor or kneeling, communicating greatness or aptitude. And when it is from top to bottom it is called Contrapicado or Tilt Down is composed from high angles, it can be recorded climbing from a chair or ladder holding the camera on the shoulder communicates depth and is usually used to introduce changes of location outdoors.

- · Crane or Dolly: This movement can be done on rails placed on the ground and also by aerial crane. Its movement obliquely regularly so it is characterized by the aberrant plane.

When the movement is made following a host or presenter is called traveling. When the movement is towards a stage or landscape it is called Dolly In when the camera moves forward. When the camera on a tripod or rails is moved backwards it is called Dolly Back.

- · Lens zooms: Also known as Zoom In and Zoom Out, are the movements of the same camera lens that open or close the camera's diaphragm. Zoom In is the lens movement from a medium plane to a smaller detail of the object.

- Zoom out is the opposite lens movement, that is, it starts from a small detail of a lens to then expand and show full.

NARRATIVE LANGUAGE

Although to the sequence of Planes: Long Shot or Long Shot (LS), to the medium plane (PM) and to the closed Plane are considered a fundamental introduction, it should not be followed rigidly and also there is no rule to use those three basic shots. The visual effect will determine the sequence.

For example, in cinematographic language we work from the filming the edition where direct messages are perceived through the sequences. The sequence PL-PM-PC is satisfactory. To increase the interest gradually the PL-PM-PC-PCE sequence is more appropriate. To print suspense to a scene is a technique of Hitchcock the famous and imitated sequence PC-PC-PC-PA where the desperate face expresses doubt of its contour.

THE THIRD RULE IN PHOTOGRAPHY

During filming, the director or cameraman must manage his shots according to the frame of the Rule of Thirds.

This rule is very simple. Divide with four imaginary lines all framing into three vertical sections and three horizontal sections, where the points of convergence serve as a guide to focus a group of two or more people talking, leaving enough lateral air with respect to their position and to whom they speaks.

THIRD RULE

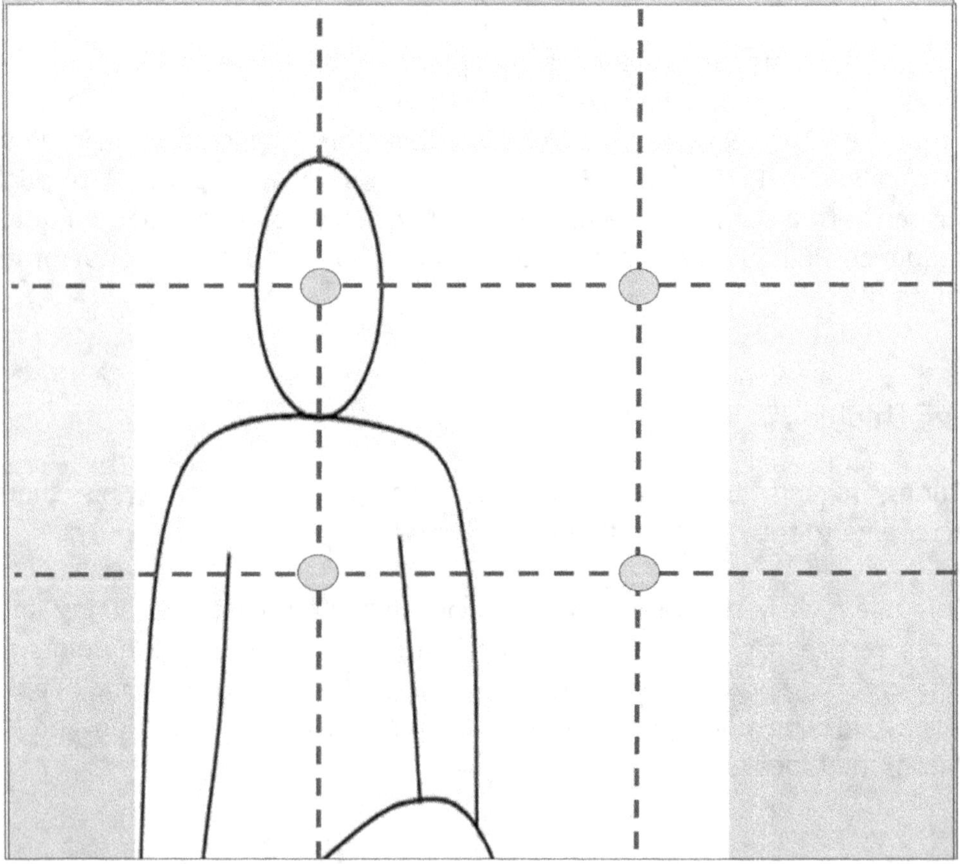

In this graph we observe how the points of convergence serve as a guide to focus the approach of the subject within a group of two or more people conversing, leaving enough lateral air with respect to their own position and that of the other subject to whom he speaks.

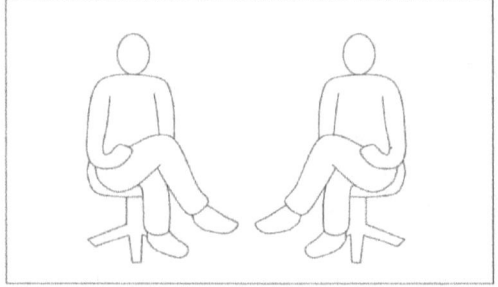

It should be remembered when making static shots of people, frame the shot so that it leaves enough space in the direction the person is looking. The result will be logical and comfortable for the viewer, reinforcing the direction in which the subject looks.

Audio and sound

During Production, the audio director or Audio Engineer, in the locations of the filming and in the sound studio, works with one or several assistants such as the Sound Editor, who is responsible for pre-editing the sound. The Bumper that holds the microphone reed to the actors during the action is another assistant of the sound department. These take the audio clips of:

- · Dialogues: Parliaments interpreted directly from the script.
- · Incidental sounds (Wild Tracks): They are the ones produced by the actors themselves when interacting with the sound props.
- · Sounds of Environments (Room tunes): There must be silence in the location, without bustle of third parties. Of duration of a minute that includes the change of hours and serve to match sonorous potholes of each location.
- · Sound effects (FX): These are sounds that due to their complexity must be produced with instruments for domestic use, and others, in addition to being modulated and amplified.

The musicalization is in charge of a Musical Editor who from the sessions of "page to page" or reunited with the director; they decide what will be the soundtrack or sound track of the film and the needs of each scene, as well as the background music of the initial and final credits. In some cases the director may not want to add music to his Movie or leave it a single piece of music for the end depending on his budget. Music in the public domain can be 50 years after the death of the author. In this they intervene:

- · composer,
- · singer,
- · Arranger
- · And record label or musical company.

The musical genre must be appropriate to the art design of the plot, such as a social theme film that carries urban genre music, a cultural environment includes classical instrumentals, a romance is musicalized with ballads, folk or ethnic music fits with dramas and documentaries , etc.

There are relationships between sound information and characters that are theoretically recognized as auricularisation:

1. Zero Headset for cases in which the soundtrack is subjected to the apparent distance of the character to the camera,
2. secondary internal earphone when the soundtrack appears as filtered through a character,
3. Sound subjectivity is constructed thanks to the assembly or the visual field, in such a way that the sound can be sent to a profilmic instance,
4. The primary internal auricularization will occur when certain deformations appear that separate the soundtrack from realism and refer to the subjectivity of a listening.

LOCATION AND SOUND REGISTRATION

It is during the location scouting that they must foresee all possible complications at the time of recording and filming. Some problems that are reported during filming is the reverberation, which is the persistence of the sound after the extinction of the sound source due to the multiple reflected waves that continue to reach the ear. Example of these polluting noises that should be avoided are:
- · Indoor air conditioning, refrigerators, fans,
- · The sounds of animals,
- · Zinc roofs when it rains,
- · Alarms of all kinds,
- · Airplanes in flight in airport areas,
- · Bustle of public areas,
- · Types of floor and footwear used by the actors.

Double wooden panels, rubbers, adhesive tapes and carpets are the best insulating techniques used during the tests and recordings.

That is why the environments are really built. It is called reverberation time to the interval that elapses between the moment in which a sound stops emitting and that in which its physical intensity has become a million times greater (that is, its sound has decreased by 60 decibels). The main causes that determine the bad acoustics of a room are the concentration of sound waves at certain points and reverberation. The reverberation time of a room depends on the absorption of its walls; When these are very absorbent, time is small and the room is said to be deaf.

SOUND WAVES AND THEIR CHARACTERISTICS

The crests and the valleys are those places where the transverse movement is maximum. A wave of sound, however, is composed of longitudinal movements of the air molecules - movements back and forth in the direction of wave motion - which constitutes a series of successive compressions and rarefactions. The wavelength is the distance between two consecutive compressions or rarefactions.

Sound waves produced in the larynx by the exit of the air (expiration) that, when crossing the vocal cords, makes them vibrate. The voice is defined in terms of tone, quality and intensity or strength. The optimal or most appropriate tone for speech, as well as its range of variation, depends on each individual and is determined by the length and mass of the vocal cords. Therefore, the tone can be altered, varying the pressure of the exhaled air and the tension on the vocal cords. This combination determines the frequency at which the strings vibrate: the higher the frequency of vibration, the higher the tone. Another aspect of the voice is resonance. Once it originates, it resonates in the chest, throat and oral cavity. The quality of the voice depends on the resonance and the way in which the vocal cords vibrate, while the intensity depends on the resonance and the vibration force of the strings.

Each musical instrument produces a characteristic vibration. The vibrations propagate through the air forming sound waves that reach the ear and allow us to identify the instrument even if we do not see it. The four examples shown represent waveforms typical of some common instruments. A tuning fork generates a pure sound, and vibrates regularly with a rounded waveform. A violin generates a clear sound and a toothed waveform. The flute generates a soft sound and a relatively rounded waveform. The tuning fork, the violin and the flute play the same note, so the distance between the maximums of the wave is the same in all wave forms. A gong does not vibrate on a regular basis like the first three instruments. Its waveform is jagged and random, and usually you can not recognize the note.Another important aspect of the acoustics of a room is the isolation of unwanted sounds. This is achieved by carefully sealing any slit that can pass through the sound, using thick walls and building several unattached partitions separated by air chambers.

To assess the acoustic properties of rooms and materials, scientists use instruments such as anechoic chambers or sound level meters. The anechoic chamber is a room free of echoes and reverberations, in which all the sound is absorbed by fiberglass pyramids placed on the surface of the walls and ceiling. A sound level meter measures sound sensation or physiological intensity, which is not proportional to physical intensity (energy flow per unit of time).

The meter expresses the result in decibels (dB), a logarithmic unit that is defined from a certain threshold physical intensity, I_o, in such a way that the number of decibels of a sound of intensity I is: $n° dB = 10 \lg (I / I_o)$.

The measurement of sound is classified from sub sonic to ultrasonic, and from sub to medium. During the entire shoot once the console is set, it is recommended to maintain the same volume. The previous console setting is recorded based on the peak in the voice record of the protagonist (s) which then decays and must not be lower than (-2).

THE AUDIO AND SOUND EQUIPMENT

In the normal mechanical-electronic sound recording system, the sound waves are inevitably distorted and pick up noise from the recording process itself. In digital recording these problems do not exist. The digital recorder measures the waves thousands of times per second and assigns a numerical value or digit to each of these measurements. These digits become a stream of electronic pulses that are stored in a memory for subsequent conversion and reproduction. In recent years these techniques have been used in a limited way for the production of conventional gramophone recordings. Currently, direct digital recordings are made, in which the electronic pulses are placed on a compact disc (CD), in which, observed through a microscope, they resemble a signal spiral in Morse code. The CD, once removed from its plastic case, is placed in a computer where a laser beam reads the encoded information and a series of circuits convert it into analog signals for playback through conventional speaker systems.

Among the new digital devices that have become portable and lighter is the "Handy Recorder" with two microphones to record environments. Measure the level of the sound signal, with a pair of inputs or jacks for headphones. It is recorded in a range between 12 - 3. Where 30 is a range of noise. It has the ability to create folders or folders with files of type .wav (Waveform audio) and mp3 as an option compressed in memory.

This device allows side inputs via USB cable, volume, headphones, hold and power on.

The use of the clapper until today continues being necessary to synchronize audio and video. As part of the main equipment we have a sound source, collector, 3 analog signals, cables and connectors available to the technician or field electricians.

TYPES OF MICROPHONES

Three types of microphones are used in television and film shooting:

- · Dynamics: Dynamic microphones include ribbon microphones and mobile microphones. The first ones have a thin metallic tape attached to the diaphragm, placed in the bosom of a magnetic field. When the sound wave hits the diaphragm and vibrates the tape, a small voltage is generated by electromagnetic induction. The operation of the moving-coil microphone is based on the same principle, but it has a coil of fine wire instead of a ribbon. Some modern microphones, designed to capture only unidirectional sounds, carry a combination of tape and coil.

- · Condenser: Another type is the condenser microphone. It has two thin metal sheets very close, which act as a condenser. The back sheet is fixed, while the previous one acts as a diaphragm. The sound waves modify the distance between the sheets, altering the electrical capacitance between them. If a microphone of this type is integrated into the corresponding circuit, the variations can be amplified and produce an electrical signal. This type of microphones are usually very small. In the hearing aids, another very common type is used, the electret condenser microphone.

- · Crystal: Another very common variant, the crystal microphone, uses piezoelectric crystals, in which a voltage is created between the two faces of the crystal when a pressure is applied. In this type of microphone the sound waves vibrate a diaphragm that in turn modifies the pressure on a piezoelectric crystal, which generates a small voltage that is later amplified.

In cinematography the Bumper or cane, or aluminum hanger is used. It must be placed in the correct position both the rod and the microphone, holding it with both arms and locate the position of the microphone in front of the speaker. Depending on the position and distance, the cane rests on the wrist or shoulders of the sound engineer.

Other recommendations are:

- · Prevent the shadow of the microphone in the camera from being reflected.
- · Sponge or speck should be used outdoors when there is too much wind to avoid reverberation.
- · A box indicated by the director that limits his range of mobility respecting that of the camera must be marked on the scene area.
- · The 48 - 24 standard is the pulse on which the recorder runs.

AUDIO EDITION

As the "folies" or audio files are obtained, the audio director with the help of a Data manager must organize, as the sound design was done separately, the types of files such as music, sounds, environment, etc. These can be numbered and colored by groups such as: Voice 1, Voice 2, Dialog 1, Dialog 2, Effect 1 ...

Sometimes ambient sounds are used to match dialogues in the same scene. This will be delivered to the director of assembly when it passes to Post production.

The digital edition today is done through softwares in a dual way. The best known are "Pro Tools 10" and "Premier" through various formats such as .aaf, .omf and .qt. Which every 6 centuries adds a bit and synchronizes the OMF file. It works by numbered track, start to finish stopwatch, duration and wave graph, among other options and configurations.

The voice over and outside screen are mounted from the studio another day. Regarding the fulfillment of the script, there are things that by distance are obviated or on the contrary by their importance are indicated to the actor during the action.

The pre-mix is also maintained through Sound mixer that can be around $ 2 thousand dollars. There is a process of "debugging" the sound before it is approved by the director and the sound is assembled. There may be several people in charge of reproducing the sounds according to the budget of the movie.

The mixes in Film and Television are different. In TV they are compressed to achieve the analogous conversion that the medium still maintains. While in cinema the mastering of music and dialogues is sent internationally, for example to Chile and others.

Pre Edition and Data Managing

He is a professional in computer science and programming. For example Movie Magic is a program that throws the shooting plan. It is the only software used in the international film industry, which assigns colors to the schedules by location.

Memory is made up of chips that store information that the CPU needs to recover quickly. Random access memory (RAM) is used to store the information and instructions that operate computer programs. Generally, programs are transferred from a disk drive to RAM. This memory is also known as volatile memory because the information contained in the memory chips is lost when the computer is disconnected. The read-only memory (ROM) contains crucial information and software that must be permanently available for the operation of the computer, for example the operating system, which directs the actions of the machine from startup to disconnection. ROM is called non-volatile memory because ROM memory chips do not lose their information when the computer is disconnected.

Electricity

The Gaffer or Head of electricity in a set of recording of a film, is in charge next to the Producer of Field, or to the Head of Floor in the case of the television, to install and to guarantee the sources of electricity for the machinery of equipment of sound , lights and cameras that will operate in the exterior locations of the film.

The Best Boy is the electricity assistant. Depending on the complexity of the production, a group of electricians called juicers are hired.

Film Direction

He is the key person in the making of a movie. It is who converts a script into images, and for that, all those involved in the project are at their command: the technical team and the artistic team, made up of the actors. Their work does not start on the first day of filming, but much earlier from development and pre-production. Together with the production manager, he draws up a shooting plan that decides the division of the film into locations and shots from the script. The director prints a personal style to the film, and the success or failure of it depends to a large extent on his work.

It is from the Director that the orders that allow the film to assume its own form must be split. Among the most important skills that are considered must have found:
- · Organizational capacity.
- · Know the details of the scenario.
- · Guide the interpretation of the actors in order to obtain the best results.
- · Control all phases of filming and assembly.
- · Supervise the technical and artistic professionalism of many people.
- · Achieve a specific communicative and expressive goal.
- · Know how much to choose from each of your collaborators.

The director must endure during the performance in a mental state curiously elastic and yet firm. In the end he is the one who sums up all the decisions that are adopted in the process of narrating the argument.

Some recommendations for the director are:

- · Never try to be egocentric, or stand out more than others in the movie.
- · Never allow the editor to be inside the set during filming as he could intervene in the work of the editor.
- · Never trust your first three scripts, if you think the budget is a barrier, there are many successful examples of movies that cost less than you think.
- · Never obese characters leaving them with little dramatic force within the approach of the scenes.
- · Never trust censorship for the final work of your film, if you use foul language or excess of violence there must be two versions of the scene that will allow you to expand your audience and avoid possible limitations of being exhibited.

THE ATTENTION OF THE SPECTATOR

The objective of making a film is to capture the attention of the spectators, creating a unique space and time that arise from the joint task of all the departments and directors that work for the film.

To consider the viewer's gaze we will dwell on the way in which the elements previously seen are present in the film, which necessarily leads us to the problem of space and time.

- · The spectatorial gaze is materially forced to follow a direction stipulated by the existing interaction between the two-dimensional composition and the represented effect of three-dimensionality.
- · The gaze moves guided by certain movements, colors, distribution and sizes. A mobile element will attract more attention than a static element.
- · The distribution and size of the elements also direct the viewer's gaze.

The spatial depth is created by the relationship of two elements, size and movement. That is what is defined as different planes of depth in a frame. Temporality plays an important role in the staging. Only the very short-term plans allow us to look at the entire composition at the same time. In general, however, simultaneity must be apprehended successively. Watching a plane consumes time. Temporality, then, can be used as a fundamental element to guide the concentration of our gaze.

TIME AND CINEMATOGRAPHIC SPACE

The duration of a movie can be from 1 to 2 hours and a half in exceptional cases, as it happens with some movies.

The relationship between represented time and diegetic time has several characteristics such as:
- · Summary that is the duration of a speech shorter than that of the events represented.
- · Rhetorical figures are those designed to compress the time of the story (clock, calendar sheets that pass, written dates, voice of the narrator, etc.), with an unreal speed increase with respect to reality.
- · The ellipsis implies the elimination of a more or less broad part of the history that is considered useless for the purposes of the narrative economy. Which can be defined or undefined.
- · Planes-Sequence. Match between the diegetic time and the time represented.
- · Temporal lengthening The time of the speech can be longer than the one of the history, (decrease of speed, frame-stop (freezing of the frame).

It is timeless handling involves the presentation of an order that makes reference to the discourse can resituate the events of history to your liking.
1. Coincidence between the order of history and discourse
2. Anachronies:

- · Flasblack. When the speech breaks the flow of history to remember previous events.
- · Flashforward When the speech leaps forward.

Any anachronism can be measured in terms of distance (time between now and the jump forward or backward).

Because of its amplitude (the duration of anachronism as such). So it is impossible to elucidate the chronological relationship between the time of the story and the time of the speech.

Temporary aspects that have to do with frequency:
- · Singularity - A single discursive presentation of a moment in history.
- · Multiple Singularity - Several representations, each belonging to similar moments, but different from the story.
- · Repetition implies several discursive representations of the same moment.
- · The iteration involves a narrative presentation of various moments in the story.

On the other hand, the espacilidad denote some phenomena or assumptions:
- Events happen in specific places.
- History and story can manipulate space from the point of view of seriality.
- The film can also use, apart from the space of the story and the space of the diegesis, the physical space of the frame as a narrative element.
- Many dialogical anecdotes do not specify where the action takes place.

THE CINEMATOGRAPHIC AND STYLE LANGUAGE

If you love the hundred and want to direct a short film or feature film, you must be a good observer and activate your creative wealth to become a good director of the big screen. Achieving this requires a clear awareness and identity regarding the world of cinema around the world and also develops an intuitive understanding of what drama is.

The way in which each director combines the elements or audiovisual tools that make up the cinema, are those that define his style. These elements elements of photographic composition are usually the shooting format, digital or 35mm film, your own technical script and the types of shots, the moments when you decide to use the frame, angles, movements, and the use of techniques of lighting.

These are "Codes" that refer exclusively to the photographic composition or planning from two different points of view such as the one that refers to the delimitation of the edges and the format of the film image:

- · Format - normally rectangular with a high-wide relation. The format implies having a different surface to distribute the elements.
- · Technical script: Sometimes made based on dialogue continuity, enriched with all kinds of indications for filming and staging: list of the size of the plans (PP, PC, PM, PML, PG, etc.), shooting angles (chopped, shot, etc.), camera movements (panning, forward, backward, elevation, etc.) optical movements (forward, backward zooms), visual relationships (cut, cast, chained fades) , etc.), types of objectives used (focal, special filters), etc.
- · Representative function of the frame that consisted in marking the limits of the frame. It means separating it from the context established by the other frames.

The filming technique involves choosing a fragment of space leaving other parts out of the viewer's field of vision.

Where the field and the out of field are related:

- · Through its inputs and outputs of characters or objects and the inquiries made to the out of field.

- · With the raccord of looks as a privileged way, and the determination of the space off through the fragmentation of characters or objects.
- · The out of field delimited by the frame consists of six segments.
- · The out of field as the set of elements that, without being included in the field, are related to it by any means.

And the one that does it to the mode of realization of the image, way of looking at it, or what is the same, to the shape and scale of the planes, to the inclination of the camera and to the angulation. This is how everything refers to the typology of the plan, the exercise of style and the simple choice.

Photography is a medium that defines how a story is best told through images. All these movements are technical procedures, but they involve meaning effects. In effect, they all imply a relational function.

Every plane defines a field, understood as the portion of imaginary space contained inside the frame.
- · The frame is presented as the boundaries of the field.
- · The frame forms the basic element from which the plastic composition of the field can be structured.
- · Depth of field - effect that in cinema or in photography, arises from the correlation of a series of technical parameters, focal distance, opening of the diaphragm and serves to designate the part of the field in which the objects or people located in it are perceived with clarity.

For this reason, each of the plane types fulfill a different significant function, according to the set in which they are integrated.

The fcatores that affect the creation of a palono are the following:
  - Size - Inaccurate classification (PP, PM, PG, etc.)
  - Duration - Plane-sequence.
  - Distance - normal, wide angle, telephoto, etc.
  - Mobility

- Fixed plane
- Planes in motion
- movement of the image represented redistribution, hierarchy of elements.
- Camera movements
- Real movement of the camera.
- movement of the camera (traveling, dolly, crane)
- on its vertical-horizontal axis (panoramic)
- Movement as an apparent effect (Zoom)

As for the angulation and inclination of the camera these codes are responsible for organizing how and from where the camera to shoot. And they can be:

· Cancellation - normal, chopped and contrapicado.
· Tilt of the camera - normal, tilted to the right or to the left.

Finally the lighting influences the message that is projected through the screen with the following parameters:

o · Neutral - serves only so that the frame is perceived clearly.
o · Dramatic and compositional function.
o · Lighting works as a rhetorical device of staging according to its quality, direction, source and color.
o · Quality - refers to the intensity.
o · Direction of light - refers to the place from which it arises and is projected onto the object present in the frame.
o · Source - can be diegetic or non-diegetic, realistic or unrealistic.
o · Can be used to color naturalist or stylistically a frame.
o · These elements configure both the composition and the significant character of a plane or the film in its entirety.

First Assistant

Normally one or several management assistants are assigned, according to the budget and the complexity of the production. The first assistant controls the fulfillment of the work plan, which is prepared each day and approved by the production manager and the director; he also works with him during the shooting, helping him in the preparation of each shot.

It can be considered that within the industry the role of the First Assistant Director maintains a certain polyvalence, since it can assume several functions, depending on the criterion of the director himself. For example, in a low-budget movie, a first assistant can charge up to $ 1,500 or more for doing the work of three people in various stages of the project.

Organize the necessary copies and documentation for the directors and their assistants, who find highlighters, pens and other office material for the entire crew.

He is aware of the progress of the set and the costumes and that the necessary materials for its realization are purchased. Sometimes utility props can also be made by each department manager or made the first assistant director. It is also responsible for analyzing the script and break it down according to their costs.

Determine problems with the locations, the fulfillment of the lunches and lunch schedules, check the weather forecast, considering what will be the simplest or leave the complicated for the end of the day.

This does not mean that you can direct, although in extreme cases where it is necessary that the live is in two locations on the same day, you can assume the directions of the director in one of these. It also organizes the call sheets of actors or leave this work to the second assistant.

Second assistant

The second assistant helps the first by arranging the actors and the technical team in the right place and at the required time. He also directs the figuration (the extras), and takes care of the small details for the preparation of the work plan for the next day.

You can perform two tasks at the same time as the camera or the continuist where the budget or type of production organization merit it.

Continuity

Continuity in television series and films is very important because it is the person who is responsible for recording all the action that is carried on the set to be guides or photos, and resume the scenes of the previous day without errors of any kind.

The Continuista must know the script and the management of the different time jumps in the line of continuity of all the events of the argument. If the assembly regulates the assembly of the planes to form the unit of the film, and being all flat a space-time unit whenever there is a change from one plane to another, it will reproduce a relation between the parameters of both planes that leads to what Burch called the spatiotemporal articulation.

- · Rigorous continuity
- · Ellipsis defined and measurable
- · Indefinite ellipsis
- · Defined backspace
- · Reverse indefinite
- · Spatial articulation between two contiguous planes:
- · Simple spatial discontinuity - spatial continuity with or without temporal continuity.
- · Normal spatial discontinuity.
- · Raccord - The privileged instrument destined to weld that discontinuity.

When making a film, the plans are not filmed following the plot consecutively. The shots are not consecutive like the script, but the convenience of time and location is sought. It would waste a lot of time taking the equipment from one place to another.

- · It is expensive to have the actors all the time.
- · The locations must be close and reserved all the time of filming.
- · Therefore, the script must be broken down following a shooting plan.

Save time by grouping all the plans that have to be made from a camera position, regardless of whether they are in order according to the story or not. This way you do not need to move the camera from one side to the other between planes and the lighting needs a minimum of adjustments.

DOCUMENTATION OF CONTINUITY

Finally, the organization that relates the Continuista according to the volume and complexity of its project can format its own Continuity Sheets which have the precise data of the entire shoot:

- · For the filming unit. It is necessary to have a record of the filming and also of what each shot consists of, in order to preserve the continuity between different planes, independently of the filming order.

- · What happens in each shot, the relationship between dialogs, position of the accessories, etc. Everything the camera sees must be recorded in order to have references.

- · The camera needs technical notes, lenses, distance or filters.

- · For the editor You are interested in knowing the number of the clapperboard, the description of the shot, the good shot, etc.

Directing Theory

From the theory of communication to narrative, we can cite a variety of authors who have contributed to the study of semiotics and other branches related to the development of media and multimedia. For Benveniste, language has two modes: the semiotic, characteristic of the sign, and the semantic, proper to discourse. The semiotic mode refers to the isolated units of the language, considered out of context and without reference when they are available for use. The semantic mode is based on the statements and, therefore, entails the existence of references to the real world. Benveniste contributed in a crucial way to the theory of communication. His distinction between semiotics and semantics was intended to complement the definition of Saussure's sign, which offered no link between the sign and its use in discourse, or between the sign and the world of which it is a part. All narrative text, parallel to what happened with the signs, articulates an expression (speech) with a content (story) or, more specifically, a form of expression with a content form. The production process of a film is based on the ability to control and control different techniques with a greater or lesser degree of specificity. Some belong strictly to the cinematographic field (filming, editing), but others, although each in its own way, are shared by other artistic activities (artistic direction and interpretation, but also personnel management or work organization) .

In France, André Bazín in his film Specifity theory pointed out that the "Sequence plane with depth of field, an alternative to classical montage that allows an exemplary fusion of narrative realism and perceptual realism". He also mentions that "Cinema would be constituted in a synthetic, more realistic and more intellectual language", a statement that we have been able to corroborate today.

The director of Russian cinema and theater Sergei Mikhailovich Eisenstein considered the cinema a kind of political weapon when writing in his work "Theory and cinematographic techniques": "The ambiguity of reality, it was necessary to combat it, avoiding the confusion of the cinematographic image with a immediately realistic capture of the world. "

Result of this neorealist ideology is expressed in director Passolini's film, entitled "120 Days of Sodom" which is an adaptation of The Republic of Saló written by him Marques de Sade.

In the world there are also authors that are cited to interpret the theory of cinema. The necessarily selective character of the cinematographic narrative, which obliges all discourses to choose which events and actants to show and which ones to maintain implicit, establishes a series of relations between the diegetic time (or time of the story) and the time represented (time of the discourse), which can be analyzed in terms of order, duration and frequency (Genette, 1972).

Román Gubern points out that the syntagmatic operation of the montage (selection and arrangement of spatio-temporal fragments) reproduces the conditions of selectivity of human perception and memory, in what they have of discontinuity and of privileging certain significant aspects to the detriment of others that they are not.

Another of the great Russian theorists was Konstantin Sergeyevich Stanislavski who was an actor, director and author of "An actor prepares" who was a pioneer in preparing actors said: "The important thing is not to lose sight of the expected arrival point. "Each character and his action in a plot script contain a specific but partial objective, which should not contradict the general character of the work". The term "super-objective" is taken from this great Russian theatrical director Stanislavski. In the same way that when we develop a conflict in a script, we have an objective -or a super-objective- that is to get somewhere, and we have a motivation: we want to get there, these two extremes will allow us to draw a line that will unite them, but at the same time It will also allow us to analyze the well-founded nature of the choice of one or the other point of the journey.

The French scriptwriter Jean-Claude Carriere cited as a historical example two different ways of structuring a story.
1. In the oriental narrative: Chinese, Indian, Arabic and as examples in Spanish literature, such as "El lazarillo de Tormes". This type of structure develops a sort of linear description like that of a journey from one place

to another, in the course of which various episodes occur in which the protagonist is linked to people who in turn tell their story and so on.

2. The dramatic tragedy that was born in ancient Greece and had its heyday in the seventeenth century France and that extends into the Western tradition to this day, where the story begins unfolds and culminates following a progression that opens and closes a conflict .

Carriere concluded by saying that these two great traditions sometimes come to mix.

KEY IDEAS OF THIS CHAPTER

▶The day of filming a film begins with the technical area: installation of electricity wiring, awnings, equipment of audio, scenographies and lights. All this in charge of the Field Producer or Field Producer that is in charge of set up an appropriate space for the rest of the crew.

▶The artistic side then appears to prepare to start shooting. The Actors are served in dressing rooms improvised by the assistant directors, makeup artists and costume designers; while they review for the last time their dialogues Right in the middle of the day everything must be arranged so that the director indicates lights, camera and action. The Data manager will keep save the valuable audio and video clips.

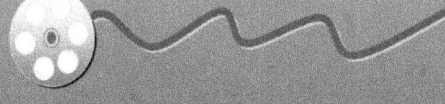

1. ▶A filming plan can cover 6 to 10 weeks, if it is a feature film or less than a week if it is a short film. Is a period of intense work production, where every detail is planned to be arranged at a time of accurate shooting, with trained personnel to obtain the best result.

SUGGESTED ACTIVITIES

VISION OF MOVIES: Select the behind the scenes or Making of several movies. Discuss in group your doubts and comment in class about the various details of your production.
SHORT FILM: Perform one or two short films in a group:
1. Choose the best short film script, written with the purpose of keeping it within a low budget:
2. Accessible locations and few actors.
3. Perform the tasks of casting, budget, scenography and props. Organize previous tests.
4. Perform the technical script and the shooting.

CHAPTER 8

POST PRODUCTION AND EDITING

- ► Editing Techniques
- ► Artistic edition
- ► Advertising edition
- ► Editing sequences
- ► Mastered movies
- ► Film Marketing Plan
- ► Film Distribution Plan
- ► Collection and rights

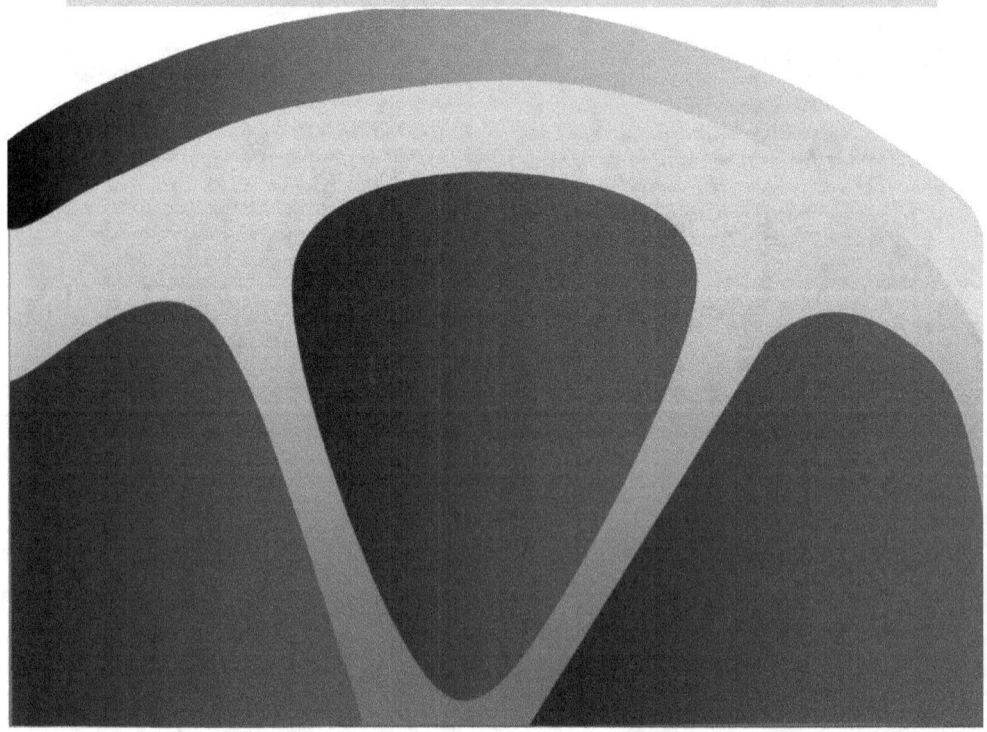

POST Production

The editing of the digital version of a director's opera prima is the end of several long-term efforts, but it is the beginning of the best stage of the movie. It is just when the advertising promotion of the premiere of the work is organized in movie theaters, where an audience interested in enjoying its unique plot, and being part of the great local and international industry. It is the moment when you will finally know how entertaining, exciting and meaningful can be your story. It is an enriching experience that carries lessons for everyone.

A film is the assembly of hundreds of short shots, so its arrangement in a sequence that takes place, rhythmically, and without sudden changes, is a specialized art. This function is fulfilled by the assembler, or assemblers, who supervise the teams of specialists in the cutting and assembly of both the soundtracks and the negative of the image.

The editor synchronizes the image with the sound (task usually entrusted to the assembly assistant). Watch the daily shots with the director and the key members of the team (the director of photography, who supervises his own work). Today, many movies are mounted on video, and then that montage serves as a reference for cutting and splicing the celluloid negative. The preparation of these daily shots takes place every day throughout the filming of the film. Postproduction is the moment in which the assembler has gathered all the necessary material to complete a first montage of the film. After the director and the producer approve the final assembly, a specialized sound editor corrects the possible problems with it. If necessary, the sound editor re-recorded the dialogues in a recording studio, while the actors see the corresponding image in projection. This process is known as dubbing. Sound editors gather the recordings and sometimes create new sounds (sound effects) to intensify the dramatic force of a scene. While the soundtrack is being prepared, the editor also monitors the optical effects and titles that will be incorporated into the film. One of the final steps is the preparation and mixing of the different soundtracks in a single master, first magnetic, which will contain the dialogues, music, direct sound and sound effects, synchronized with the image and appropriate to the volume of each band. The mixing without the dialogues makes possible the dubbing for the distribution of the film in other languages.

The edition is defined as a concept of spatial and temporal union, it is something that cinematography borrowed from other arts such as photography, painting and literature, where the union of actions provides the reader with logical continuity in the animation of the story as well as the creation of an idea.

Editing Techniques

How to show scenes that happen simultaneously? For this there are several possibilities:
1. Showing actions that coexist in the same field (for example, thanks to the depth of field).
2. That they coexist in the same frame (double exposure).
3. Present them in succession.
4. Present them in alternate assembly.

The types of edition or assembly are:

- · Alternating Assembly - proposes a wide series of analepsies or setbacks, defined two events simultaneously and diegetically distant in space.
- · Parallel Assembly - In which the actions that are shown alternately are not simultaneous at the time of the story.
- · Convergent Assembly - physical separation of groups in conflict that converge towards a single place in a single time.

The first films of the LUMIERE brothers, were of a single picture, in them the assembly or the union of tape was absent. Over time, there was a need to extend the Films because a large number of actions and events could not be filmed in a single frame and it was necessary to "paste" the different shots that had previously been filmed separately. The purely technical union of two different paintings was the first form of primitive editing and was called TECHNICAL ASSEMBLY

THE ASSEMBLY PRINCIPLE

One of the most obvious features of cinema is that it is an art of combination and disposition. This feature is what essentially characterizes the idea of montage and we can point out at the outset that this is a central idea in any theorizing of the filmic fact.

The assembly in a film (and usually in the cinema) is first of all a technical work, organized as a profession, and that in the course of a few decades of existence has established and progressively set certain procedures and certain types of activity.

- · Let's quickly remember how the chain that leads from the script to the finished film is presented in the case of a traditional production:
- · A first stage is to break down the script into units of action and, eventually, to break them down to obtain filming units (planes).
- · These shots during shooting generate several shots.

The set of these takes constitutes the "rushes", from which the assembly work itself begins, which consists of three indispensable operations:

1. A selection, among the "rushes", of the useful elements (those that are rejected constitute the discards).
2. A linking of selected planes in a certain order (thus obtaining what is called a "first continuity").
3. Finally, the exact length that should be given to each plane and the junctions (raccords) between these planes is determined with a precise level.

The assembly consists of three major operations: selection, combination and splicing. These three operations are intended to achieve, from separate input elements, a totality that is the film.

DEFINITION OF THE CONCEPT

The purpose and function of the edition is given by the need to expose the theme organically and coordinated, in addition to the content, the plot, the action, the movement within the film series and its dramatic action as a whole from the animation of a fable and even its logic and continuity. Other definitions indicate:

- · Assembly: Series of codes that articulate the process of composition and meeting of all the elements to build the film.
- · Assembly: Operation designed to organize the set of planes that form a film according to a predetermined order. It is therefore an organizational principle that governs the internal structure of visual and / or sound filmic elements.

The film is composed of separate portions of tapes that together make up the representations, the actions, the images, the events, the episodes, the dramatic structures and the whole.

BASIC ELEMENTS OF THE EDITION

During the editing process two fundamental aspects are joined by juxtaposing two or more tables:
1. Content of the shot
2. the time that passes in each table

TECHNICAL SCREEN AS THE BASIS OF THE EDITION

The technical script is the basis of the edition, in which are described the different shots and angles of the camera, as well as the duration of each frame. The technical script is unfilmed literature, it is the most approximate literary idea of how the future audiovisual work will be (wedge, film, documentary)

According to Russian theorists, the two major editing methods are:
1. The Comfortable Edition
2. The Artistic edition

COMFORTABLE EDITION

Editing is a process that must be foreseen when writing a technical script and drawing the story board, but for this a certain training of the imagination is required to feel the effect of changing the pictures on the screen. This training begins with the location of the camera in relation to the subject; what portion of the subject will be fixed by the camera and how that portion will look on the screen.

The goal of comfortable editing is that the actions that take place on the screen occur with the logic of real life without affecting the process of visual perception of the objects or subjects that participate in the action. If a subject enters the box on the left and leaves on the right the logical union with a subsequent frame is that the subject re-enters from the left and moves to the right.

If we establish a certain position for a subject A, for example, the right of the screen and during the filming we neglect the subject's position and we film it to the left, this shot can not be joined with the rest by composition since it would look like the subject will jump from right to left.

The same relationship occurs with all the subjects or objects that participate in the action at the time of filming.

ASSEMBLY OBJECTS

- Plane must be made here in only one of its dimensions, which determines the inscription of time in the film (ie: the plane characterized by a certain duration and a certain movement), and therefore as equivalent to the expression "unity (empirical) of the montage ".

But we can consider that the operations of organization and disposition that define the assembly can be applied to other types of objects:

Three types of operation:
1. juxtaposition (of homogeneous or heterogeneous elements)
2. ordination (in continuity or succession)
3. Fixation of duration

The assembly is the principle that regulates the organization of visual and sound filmic elements, or the set of such elements, juxtaposing them, chaining them and / or regulating their duration.

ASSEMBLY FUNCTIONS

1. Narrative function - The assembly ensures the linking of the elements of the action according to a relationship that, globally, is a relationship of causality and / or diegetic temporality: under this perspective, it is always

about making the "drama" better perceived and correctly understood by the viewer.

2. Expressive function, that is, one that "is not a means but an end" and that "manages to express by itself -by the clash of two images- a feeling or an idea".

- Assembly ensures, among the elements that unite, "formal" relationships, recognizable as such, more or less independent of meaning. These relationships are essentially of two kinds:
- Effects of liaison, or on the contrary, of disjunction, and more broadly, all the effects of punctuation and marking.
- Effects of alternation (or, on the contrary, of linearity).

3. Semantic functions - It covers extremely numerous and varied cases. Perhaps artificially, we will distinguish:

- the production of the denoted sense-essentially spatio-temporal-that encompasses, in the end, what the category of "narrative" editing described: montage is one of the great means of production of the filmic space, and more generally, of all the diegesis;
- the production of connoted meanings, very diverse in their nature: namely, all the cases in which the montage relates two different elements to produce an effect of causality, parallelism, comparison, and so on.

4. Rhythmic functions - The filmic rhythm is presented, then, as the superposition and the combination of two types of rhythms, completely heterogeneous:

- Temporal rhythms, which have found a place in the soundtrack (although we should not absolutely exclude the possibility of playing with durations of visual forms, and "experimental" cinema as a whole is often tempted to produce such visual rhythms);
- plastic rhythms, which can result from the organization of the surfaces in the painting, the distribution of luminous intensities, colors, etc. (classic problem of twentieth-century painting theorists such as Klee or Kandinsky).

Artistic edition

The artistic edition is the process of joining the various takes and times of the film and can have different purposes, build a parallel narrative, show an allegory, accelerate the pace of action, display images under various musical bits and even achieve tension or confusion in the viewer. Even the experimental genre, or the combination of various sub genres of cinema such as animation, stopmotion, the absence of a central plot, or juxtaphoto images can be considered within the artistic edition.

The artistic edition is the result of detailed studies on the possibilities of the juxtaposition of the paintings (although many of these rules were discovered by chance, through trial and error)

If we are presented with the scene of the painting "The Flood" by Leonardo Da Vinci, which closed well-chosen combined plans as the following:

"The shining members of the fighters appearing in full light. Challenging eyes Hands hitting the flesh when holding on tightly. Sweat smell of animalsalvaje. Paleness mixed with blond whiskers. Bruised meat flushing. Backs sweating like the stone walls of a steam bath. Advance pulling on the knees. Turning over their heads, etc. "

We will discover that in a few seconds of description the different shots that make up the "assembly elements" literally touch all the senses, except maybe the taste, present however for indifference.
1. Sense of touch: "backs sweating like the stone walls of a steam bath"
2. Sense of smell: "smell of wild animal sweat"
3. Sense of sight: This includes the light "the deep shadow and the bright limbs of the fighters appearing in full light, buttons and the fists of the swords of the police officers twinkling in the deep shadow" and the color "paleness mixed with blond whiskers, bruised flesh flushing. "
4. Sense of hearing: "hands hitting the flesh"
5. Sense of movement: "crawling on the knees, turning on their heads."
6. Emotion or drma: "challenging eyes".

Innumerable examples of this kind could be cited, but all would illustrate to a greater or lesser degree the thesis previously stated, that is: There is no fundamental difference between the paths to be followed to make a purely visual montage and a montage that unites different spheres of feeling, particularly to the visual image with the auditory image, in the process of creating a single and unifying audio-visual image.

The artistic edition is the result of detailed studies on the possibilities of the juxtaposition of the paintings (although many of these rules were discovered by chance, through trial and error).

The genres used in artistic publishing are:
- Parallel Edition
- Edition of Contrasts
- Rhythmic Edition
- Metric Edition
- Vertical Edition
- Internal edition of the painting

THE PARALLEL EDITION

Parallel actions that occur in unison in different places but that are linked by an event or a protagonist are presented. The use of parallel editing is closely linked to the presentation of memory, dreams, thoughts, and the subconscious world. The parallel edition unites different lines of action and exists in several ways:
- The parallel edition that develops through the passage of events (assembly of primitive information)
- The parallel assembly according to the course of various actions.
- The parallel assembly of sensations (Assembly of primitive comparisons).
- The parallel montage of sensations and meanings (Allegorical montage).
- The parallel assembly of representations (Assembly that builds a concept).

THE EDITING OF CONTRASTS

Two paintings that contrast because of their dramatic content; a hungry and the glutton's gluttony. The psychological mechanism has its foundation in the abrupt reconstruction of the reception process and the search for logical union between opposite phenomena.

THE METRIC EDITION

In the metric edition the dominant factor is the absolute length of each frame that is repeated in several series, such as: 2 meters + 2m + 2m + 2m + 4m + 4m + 4m + 2m or 5 frames + 7 frames + 7 frames + 7 + 7 + 10 + 10 + 10 + 5 + 5 + 5. This edition is given with an absolute calculation of the content of each frame in a determined length of time.

THE VERTICAL EDITION

In the vertical edition the images take place in conjunction with the musical chords and accents. In an orchestral score there are several pentagrams and each one contains the part of an instrument or group of instruments, each of these parts is developed horizontally, but the vertical structure plays a no less important role in relating all the elements of the instrument together. orchestra within each determined unit of time. Through the progression of the vertical line that occupies the whole and interlaced horizontally advances the intricate and harmonious musical movement of the entire orchestra. When we move from that image of the instrumental score to that of the visual score it is necessary to add something new: "A pentagram of successive visuals" that correspond, according to their own laws, with the movement of music and vice versa.

By synchronizing the music with the series, this general feeling becomes a decisive factor, since it is directly linked to both the imaginative perception of the music and that of the scenes. The vertical edition is graphically described as two lines each of which represent the complete set of a score of many voices. The search for correspondence must start with the intention of synchronizing photography and music with the complex set of audiovisual images.

THE RHYTHMIC EDITION

"The rhythm is always the most important" because in the rhythm is everything. In every moment of our life, without stopping to think about it, we live in one or another rhythm of breathing, of heart palpitations, of movement of the eyes, of a change from day to night, from destruction to creation, everything in the world is a rhythm. That's why creative work must be built on this fact - we must constantly obey by moving towards the unrepeatable rhythm of the text. It is necessary to have certainty to the last and at every moment of the correct rhythm. The rhythm is a complete whole, it is all the instrumentation of the show or the complete film, it is to move slower, to stop and it is not only the movement of the actors from one point to another of the stage but of the gestures, of a minimum turn of the head, the correlation of the actors with the stage is a part of the rhythm of the show or the film. If for example we change the angle of incidence of the light on the stage a completely different rhythm can be created for the vision.

The rhythmic edition is the correspondence between the duration of each plane and the voltage it causes in the receiver. We are not referring to an abstract rhythm in time but to a rhythm of attention. Consequently a slow pace can express a tense wait for a latent threat, hopelessness. A fast rhythm gives dynamics to the event, the process of struggle or shock when the reception can not take place calmly but is expressed through a rapid tension, a tense rhythm of the psychic process.

The rhythm of a film arises in correspondence with the character of the time that passes in each picture and is determined, not by the length of the segments joined in the montage, but by the level of tension that elapses in its time. The union of the pictures can not determine the rhythm of the film. It is precisely the time set in the box who dictates to the director one or another editing principle. That is why paintings are not united in which a different character has been fixed over the course of time. Example, real time can not join the conditional. The consistency of the time that elapses in the painting, its tension or its relaxation will be "the pressure of time" in the painting.

Consequently, assembly is a method of joining tables with a calculation of the pressure of time present in each of them.

THE INTERNAL EDITION OF THE TABLE

This type of editing is the direct result of the sequence plane. In the sequence plane the change of the torna flows through the movement of the camera, by objects or by subject.

The change of planes and their contents flow within the film series, it is to that flow of planes to what is called "internal editing of the picture".

Especial digital effets

The digital editing programs that work on any platform are based on a standard of icons and basic tasks, which

differ minimally, and which can be summarized in the following list.

The editing program in practice should cover the following aspects:
· Digital edition in Movie Magic, Movie Maker, Adobe Premiere, FINISH, and others.
· Basic characteristics of the Hardware: They are basically the equipment of a digital editing station updated as a

hard disk of high capacity between 1 terabyte or more, external disks, speakers or home theater with subwoofer technology, bass and dolby sound, high monitor definition, hearing aids, microphones, keyboard, etc.

· Basic Software Features: DVD player, Blue Ray and USB connector.
· Digital compression
· Project management within the program
· Window of Import of files to the project by Clips
· Identification of clips
· Audio tracks
· Effects and Transitions window
· Creation of dissolvences and effects
· Fade in Fade out audio
· The time Line
· Video line
· Application of division of the selected click to apply cut
· Cross Dissolve
· Titling and subtitling
· Roll or drag clips

Editing sequences

The assembly is largely a matter of experimentation. There are no rigid rules that dictate what should be done and what should not be done. However, just as there are certain principles that are useful in filming, they are also applicable to assembly and help to assemble the sequences in a coherent manner. The two most important issues - continuity and visual action - are explained by the duration of the action that takes place: example, how fast the actor approaches the door of his car.

Movies are not always mounted for visual reasons. Sometimes sound can be more important than action, especially if it is music or voices. There are also times when the mounting points of each medium come into conflict. But in general, who decides is the image obtained; a well-constructed image usually exerts an impact superior to that of any kind of comment, and therefore the action is the first thing to consider.

WHY CUT?

When projecting the film without mounting, the first thing to ask is whether a cut is really necessary. Even if you have shot a scene from different angles or have cut aways and reaction planes, it is important to decide whether your inclusion will improve or weaken the central action. Is the master plan enough? Are the angles and information provided by the other planes sufficiently different to improve the scene, or do they just complicate it without adding anything interesting? Never cut without having enough reasons or for taking advantage of the fact that you have the scene covered from several places; This is particularly true in cases where a prolonged performance or a character study has been filmed situations in which pauses and imperfections will surely say more than impeccable editing.

CHOICE OF THE CUTTING POINT

Suppose you have filmed a man who approaches a car, opens the door and leaves. He has shot the scene from three angles to have more flexibility, and he intends to cut from a general plane to a medium plane the moment he reaches the car, and to a close-up when he grabs the hand.

The action: The scene must have been shot three times: in the general plane, in the medium plane and in the foreground of the door handle.

DURATION OF THE DRAWINGS

So far we have tried the cuts between planes of the same scene although not all action cuts are intended to interconnect different camera angles of the same event. In any form of documentary film, from the familiar films upwards, it will be necessary to join planes of different moments and places whose link will be purely thematic.

Each plane will have its own rhythm, and probably a series of independent decisions throughout it. The question is, then, to find a good starting point for each case.

CHOICE OF STARTING AND FINISHING POINT

In general there are usually enough useful points to start and finish a plane. Place the film in the player, pass it a few times and look for some decisive action. As a quick gesture of a hand or the exit of a character's frame, which serves to take the view to the next plane or to dismiss the previous one; Point out the starting point and pass the plane through the player at the correct speed until you think you have located the exact place where you must finish; point it out and before giving the cut, consider the relationship with the plane that has to follow: it is very frequent that an exit movement on the left of a plane that only seemed very effective, turns out to be unsuccessful if the movement of the next one goes on opposite direction (keep in mind, however, that it is no longer a matter of continuity since they are planes of different things, but of visual effect). If all goes well, make the cut, join the next plane and study the effect of the two followed (but do not pass the film through the projector yet).

Cutting of aesthetic shoots

The search for a decisive moment of action is a procedure of determining a cut-off point but not the only one. Even more important is the time that the plan can be on screen, and that will depend in part on the overall rhythm of the sequence. Evaluating this time is particularly difficult when you are assembling a series of fixed planes or cutaways.

First, because in a fixed plane nothing happens, and therefore there is no action that facilitates things. Second, because unless a player is available, the film will almost always pass at the speed that is comfortable, not the correct one: this extreme can be controlled to a certain extent with a table of projection times that converts the footage into time in screen; however, it is best to cut the long plane in the rough assembly phase. and re-cutting during the first cut phase once the entire sequence has been passed through the projector at the correct speed.

Keep in mind that a fixed plane will have to be as much longer as more information is included. If the plane has been seen before it can be left short; but if it is a surprise or if it contains many details there will be more time on the screen. There is always the danger that as the film becomes familiar as the assembly progresses, the cuts become larger and larger.

Brindging the plane

In cinema the convention that says that any new scenario or any time lapse must be introduced by means of a situation plan is respected. In general, it is a general or medium plane in which the relative position of the persons or things that will be seen in the subsequent planes is appreciated; indicates to the audience where the action occurs, as the camera looks at the scene and perhaps also that a certain amount of time has passed since the previous scene.

This convention has, therefore, a solid practical foundation: it establishes the scene and allows cutting to closer planes, although in a long sequence it will possibly be necessary to return to it from time to time. In any case, it is possible to vary the formula to achieve a certain effect: thus, it is common in the creation of suspense to begin with a series of unconnected and inexplicable close-ups. that only at the end can be placed when the situation piano appears.

The problems of the jump of the axis have already been explained, and it is fundamental that the rules followed during the filming are still obeyed during the assembly. When assembling a series of plans the continuity of direction must be maintained, otherwise the audience will be confused.

Similar and contrasted plans

When joining two planes there are times when the succession of images chosen determines the "air" of the sequence. For example, it is possible to improve the flow of action and in some cases suggest a harmonious relationship between very diverse objects if a certain similarity is established between consecutive planes. This similarity can be of composition and even of color. On the contrary, if the composition or colors collide, the effect will be of drama and contrast. This phenomenon is a tool of great value in the establishment of rhythm and atmosphere.

And it is not the "appearance" of two consecutive planes the only thing to consider: one must also be aware of the effect of joining very moved, or fixed planes. The relation between movement and stillness is in delicate cinema and exerts a considerable effect on the final result. At one extreme, all the action could happen before a fixed camera, and in the other the camera could be constantly zooming, describing panoramas and travelings in a kind of frantic movement. In general, an intermediate effect will be pursued; Unless you want to give the feeling of great movement, you should never place a zoom or pan next to another. The moving shots must be spaced, especially if they go in the same direction, placing between fixed half planes. And in all cases it is necessary to wait until any movement that occurs in a fixed plane ends before cutting.

Think about the different choices you can make by changing the size and angle of the plane. A jump from, for example, a general shot to a first close-up will result in an excessive and very dramatic screen: the effect is very expressive if that is what you are looking for. But if something like that is introduced without a clear reason, it will be inadequate and will break the flow of action.

PROCESSING AND EDITING: Elaboration of a Sequence

When assembling a sequence, it must be remembered that the rhythm of the sequence is determined by the duration and frequency of the planes, as well as by the movement of their contents. Get used to looking at the sequences not only from the point of view of the action you develop, but also based on the rhythm. The most important point to remember is that a rapid intercalation produces tension and passion on its own. What matters is the variation of the cutting tempo, not its average speed between two points. A slow intensification followed by a sudden explosion of rapid close-ups is something much more effective than an agitated sequence full of cuts for no reason. If a sequence has to be fast, the length of the planes can be varied, including a longer one whose rhythm emanates not from its duration, but from the speed of the action it contains.

To achieve an atmosphere of calm and daydreaming, it is best to cut the planes at regular intervals, so that the variations in composition, duration and frequency of them are sufficient to overcome the weight of interest, although not so much as to alter the tranquility of the action.

To create suspense, it is possible to reach a compromise between the two previous possibilities: thus, a series of slow general plans and at the end a real violent blow. The best way to judge the rhythm of a sequence is to pass it by a motorcycle, although with practice it can also be done by hand.

Mastered movies

In cinematography, but not in television, the development of 35mm negatives continues, which is sent to the United States or Europe. The digital transfer to film has a cost of € 25,000 from where the master copy is obtained. Since the consolidation of digital cinema this practice has fallen into disuse, but the demands of filming and high-resolution editing have replaced them.

Audio synchronization is also another task prior to editing the master copy. Re-recording is the process by which the audio tracks of a movie or video production are created. As the elements of sound are mixed in the edition and combined in a necessary process the recording of all the elements of audio such as dialogue, music, sound effects to achieve the desired final result. Inclusive the soundtrack which is the song that the audience will hear once the film ends the movie seen.

Low-budget films such as "The Blair Witch Project" can have promotional costs that are much more expensive than the development.

Film Marketing Plan

In social communication, campaigns aimed at promoting an audiovisual product start from the moment the theme of the plot is chosen, the thematic genre and the filming format define the image quality at the end of the product that will be obtained. The price would be another important aspect, although the box office price in Latin America varies between each country, we could establish a range of $ 4 to $ 9, where the total of the collection is summarized with the following formula:

BOX-OFFICE COLLECTION

$ Audience / $Tickets   = $ Movie Collection
60,000   ÷ $4.90   = $ 294,000.00

It is considered that the total number of spectators captured as a general rule is lower for successful minorities.

The promotion and distribution of the film suggest an investment in companies and marketing professionals, such as services for renting and making souvenirs, sponsor banners, rugs, the number of venues where it will be premiered, advertising on open television and print media, etc. From a budget of a low budget film in independent cinema from 200 thousand to 300 thousand, approximately $ 30, 000 is separated for advertising promotion of the film.

The exchange and the procentual participation are two techniques that are added to Product placement to cover the needs of production in exchange for advertising on posters, social networks and web pages of the film, after signing agreements in which informality should be avoided, even more so when the film registers success.

Film Distribution Plan

A film production is generally "not sold" but the rights are given where the partition is shared, this according to the territory.

According to the following parameters:
- · According to a certain time.
- · It is made according to a specific amount of exhibitions, according to the price.
- · It is for certain media.
- · Clauses or conditions are also made by language.

The distribution rights of a script, considering a final percentage of the copyright of the writer are broken down as follows:
- · Cinema: Private rooms of various companies.
- · Television: Open, reserved rights of exhibition.
- · Cable TV: Pay per view, Home Video, etc.
- · Derivatives: As transferred to airlines, hotels, etc.
- · Merchandising: Internet, editorial, CD Rom, toys, textiles, and souvenirs.

In general, contracts are signed with local or international sales agents. These contracts give the right to agents to receive, for example, 25% for the sales they get. For this purpose, it is recommended at this stage to include attendance fees for Forums and festivals that have among their activities, the market of potential buyers. France with Marche du Film, AFM, Matpe, Mipcom is considered the most effective according to the region proposed.

If this type of negotiation is done with a distributor during pre-production, it is called Pre-sale, which is a type of limited distribution agreement for a specific territory before the start or end of the production of a film. It occurs under the following conditions:

- · A god willing to give an advance.
- · Will pay as a percentage based on profitability. For example, on HBO they demand that the right of exhibition on television not be assigned.

Collection and rights

The main production company will be able to create a limited representation society that represents the film before the entire signing of agreements of financial, economic and social interest. This type of company may for social interest funds ceded by government funds, foundations and private companies that are attached to the project as sponsors.

In esumidas accounts this relation is summarized as follows:
Producer ↔ Investor ↔ Exhibitors ↔ Distributors ↔ Public

The administrative office of the project must comply with all legal commitments before its closing date. The bylaws shall include at least the name of the company, the object, address and share capital, the closing date of the fiscal year and the manner of organizing the company's administration. They can be contributed or rights, but not work or services; the contributions can be monetary and not monetary.

There are taxes for exhibitions ranging from $ 200 to $ 1,000 for foreign films. For example, sometimes these commitments are not disbursed immediately, so the payments are deducted:

PAYMENT REPORT:

$ Net
- Less distribution for Special Taxes
= Collection by sale of exhibition rights

After the premiere, expenses that are discounted from a fund or capital of the total collected continue to be recorded, for example:

EXPENSES TO DATE:

$ Gross collection
- Less Print DVD's
- Movement by marketing of DVD's
- Billed shipping services
= Net collection

FILM PRODUCER PERCENTAGE

$ Collection - Less taxes = SubTotal

Less 50% - 15% Distributors - Launch = Subtotal
Sub Total - Lesss agents = Producer Total

KEY IDEAS OF THIS CHAPTER

▶The assembly of a film begins with a meticulous organization of each clip, of each correct shot for every scene. This is how the achievement of the script is guaranteed to the editor, with a synchronized and high-quality audio track quality for theaters.

▶The post-production process leaves behind the screenwriter, the technical and artistic team, where only the producer and the The director thinks about the editing logic, about where to cut and what to leave out to highlight his message.

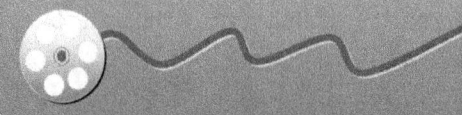

▶A marketing plan must always accompany the promotion prior to the premiere of a film, there is always possibilities to adjust the cost of the campaign according to the budget you have. Even the exhibition Free is a way to promote and stay within the industry.

SUGGESTED ACTIVITIES

DESIGN A POSTER FOR YOUR SHORT FILM: Select colors and styles of letters, a photograph taken during the filming and use it to publicize the exhibition of his short on social networks, posters and others.

SHORT FILM RELEASE: Discuss the following post-production tasks as a group:

1. Choose the best place for the short film exhibition, discuss at the end about the purpose of your argument and suggest improvements.
2. Search for calls that fit the duration, subgenre and requirements for your short film be registered and shown internationally or locally.

Glossary

1. **Dramatic action:** It refers to the events that make up the history of the film and make up a scene or sequence.

2. **Dimension:** Indication of emotion, tone or action that coexists with the words pronounced by a character, in order to complement them. The scriptwriter must write them below the name, in parentheses, before the lines of the dialogue. Dimensions usually show how the dialogue should be interpreted and it is advisable to use them only when the context may remain ambiguous.

3. **Act:** Each of the main parts in which a script can be divided. Fiction feature films, following the classical structure model, usually have three acts: The first act is the establishment or approach and has an approximate duration of a quarter of the total of the film; the second act is the act of development or knot and lasts approximately half the length of the film; and the third act is the act of denouement and lasts approximately one quarter of the final length of the film. Some TV programs are structured in two, four, seven or eight blocks; in the United States, the origin of this pattern, it is due to the fact that they are designed according to advertising cuts.

4. **Basic agreement of minimum fees:** Are the conditions in force in some countries that regulate the employment of writers and writers and are established by law.

5. **Ad Lib:** abbreviation of the Latin term "ad libitum" which means "at will" and in script is used to indicate unspecified actions and dialogues of extras present around an actor.

6. **Adaptation:** Rewrite an existing material; like for example a novel, within the format of cinematographic script. It involves

choosing which aspects of the story are adaptable, or not, to the big screen.

7. **Agent:** A professional in the film industry who helps screenwriters find work or sell their scripts. Your commission percentage is based on 10%. The author registration offices of each country govern and apply the current legislation on these works.

8. **Antagonist:** Villain or evil character who is in conflict with the main protagonist of a plot, opponent to the protagonist of the story. Normally it pursues the same goal, different intentions, or pursues a different goal opposed to that of the protagonist.

9. **Antichlimax:** It is the moment when the audience is taken to a point where the story ends leaving a feeling of dissatisfaction. Climax that does not solve the central conflict of the story, causing a disappointing feeling in the audience. Most of the time, it is an undesired effect, it happens by providing a solution too superficial, easy, incredible, uninteresting to consider a central conflict. Culminating dramatic point where the action does not reach the expected dramatic rise in tension. In certain types of Cinema it may be a desired effect, but, in general, it is not well accepted by the public.

10. **Antihero:** Protagonist who does not conform to the archetype of the accepted hero.

11. **Arc:** imaginary curve on the line of evolution of a character throughout history. It is usually characterized by the adoption or abandonment of a series of values, as a consequence of the experiences experienced in history.

12. **Argumentists:** Writers who divide the author's rights, which includes percentages of distribution by the making of chapters, characters, arguments, plots and runners, as opposed to the part corresponding to who works all those elements until the writing of the script , or the one corresponding to music and direction.

13. **Argument:** It is the story that develops in a script. Sometimes it is called the most synthetic way to summarize the story, although it is necessary to clarify that the argument does not lose its status due to the extension or form of writing.

14. **Assignment**: term used in the media to designate a task to be performed within a defined period. The synopsis introduces the story to them, offering a glimpse of the film without forcing them to devour the entire script.
15. **Atmosphere**: Tone or dimension that is added between the filming and editing of an audiovisual through music, lights, scenography, costumes and makeup. In addition to the camera angles.
16. **Avant Garde**: experimental filming outside the usual limits.
17. **B.G .**: An annotation of scenery of English origin that means "background" or atmosphere that indicates to props the scene props, are secondary to the action.
18. **Beat**: classification of the general budget of the film according to your needs and confirmed financial sources.
19. **Bible**: Document or written exposition of the parameters of a television series, which includes description of the work, tone, structure of time of duration, audience target, characters and relationship between them, description of synopsis of the chapters, as well as Other data that are considered relevant. The runway is usually accompanied by a pilot script.
20. **Biography**: The true testimony of the life of a person told in a film, television series, etc.
21. **Blockbuster**: a feature film that gets a huge sales revenue.
22. **Draft**: It is the first version of the script written continuously that includes dialogues. It is delivered to potential executives and investors during preproduction.
23. **Box office**: Sales of movie theaters.
24. **Breakdown**: Detailed shooting and analytical plan that lists all the requirements related to filming, on a daily basis, such as actors, props, costumes, etc.
25. **Letter of request**: It is a letter of a page to aspire to an agent or producer read a work, only brief and relevant information is provided.
26. **Catalyst**: It refers to an event, information or element that induces the protagonist to act in a certain direction, is an element that generates a dramatic activation.

27. **Censorship**: Review of the classification for the exhibition of a film made by a censor entity which has the authority to request certain changes before allowing its exhibition under certain classification levels.
28. **Certification of Authorship**: Legal document that legally certifies the author of a script, film or other work, establishing patrimonial rights on it through a payment of tax stamps. This procedure protects the work of possible future legal demands.
29. **Assignment of rights**: document drafted by a lawyer by trade that must be signed by the scriptwriter in exchange for an agreed amount or a future percentage on reported earnings.
30. **Contingent Compensation**: Payment that may be included as a bonus, derived earnings, reserved rights, or payment for an eventual sequel to a movie.
31. **Compensation**: Money paid to a writer for the sale of a script or for services rendered within an audiovisual production.
32. **Concept**: A unique premise that can be understood through a sentence. For example: "Blue zebras in space" (Avatar)
33. **Text corrector**: Analyst hired for the grammar correction of movie scripts.
34. **Cut to**: direction at the end of a scene indicating change of place, of a set or sequence of several scenes of the same day, or change of time.
35. **Credits**: The measurement and placement of the names of the production team and financial partners at the beginning of the film and in any related printed material.
36. **Crisis**: point in the dramatic action where everything stops when reaching the most doubtful point, it is a dramatic pause that starts the last section until the climax of the story. Before the "crisis" the protagonist is shown as it really is and his reaction to it is what usually leads to the climax.
37. **Cross-genre**: cross gender or combination of two genres, such as Horror-comedy, comedy-romance, musical-drama, drama-historical, adventure-science fiction, etc. If the case happens that the argument mixes more than two genres, its characteristics should be revised and adjusted.

38. **Culmination:** scenes from a movie where the elements of a story are then finished and the status of a character is shown after a climax.

39. **Related rights:** Dícese of the rights that due to their relationship with the creation of an original work must be subject to the same process. Call distribution rights or public exhibition in festival halls or samples of an audiovisual work, rights of reproduction of posters, logos, characters, books, making of, etc. That legally enable an author to receive a percentage of profits from his producer partner.

40. **Copyright:** Protection established on any creative expression that is fixed and tangible from books, music, finished film, etc.

41. **Development:** process in which a script is composed before filming or production in which it can be altered or modified to consider the personal vision of any executive or individual involved in the project.

42. **Description:** detail of what we see in the film, especially actions and visual aspects of the locations, characters or costumes. It is always described in the present tense and only what can be seen in the film should be captured. It is inappropriate to describe sensations, thoughts, actions to come, past actions, justifications, explanations and concepts beyond the moment itself.

43. **Outcome:** third and final act of the film, where the dramatic action culminates, all the ends are tied, the riddles are solved the questions raised throughout the film must be answered (unless a possibility is consciously chosen) alternative). The outcome contains the climax and resolution and usually answers the dramatic question.

44. **Detonant:** incident located in the first act and which determines a nine direction of the story usually by provoking or imposing a different direction to its protagonist, linked this to the central dramatic conflict that arises.

45. Deux Ex Machina: A type of resolution to the problem of an argument that is too convenient for the writer and unbelievable for the audience.

46. Director: He is the creative chief behind the workforce of a film.

47. Dissolve to: Visual direction in a script indicating that the end of a scene fades gradually over the beginning of the next scene.

48. Distributors: The biggest studios in Hollywood are MGM / UA, 20th Century Fox, Sony Pictures, Wagner Bros., Paramount Pictures, Universal and Disney.

49. Public Domain: When a work enters the public domain, it legally loses the protection of copyright, which according to each country can go from 50, 70 or 100 years after the author's death.

50. Ellipsis: It is the omission of any element that corresponds to the happenings of history. It can be an ellipsis in dialogues, the presence of a character, a scene or time itself. If it is done correctly, it prints rhythm and efficiency to the narration. On the contrary, if it is not presented in a correct way, it blurs the narrative clarity.

51. Packaging: The process by which the representatives of distribution agencies by cable and open television sign with the producer of a project and sell it to a studio, for example Paramount, and distribute it within a determined territory.

52. Escaleta: list of scenes from the script with a brief description of them, which marks the dramatic progression of the work. A full rundown takes all the scenes of the script, if intermediate splits are sometimes used, which only carry the large blocks of sequences. A very detailed outline in its description can be the origin of a sequenced treatment.

53. Scene: basic unit of the script formed by a series of pianos that form a dramatic action within the plot and that normally maintain the spatial and temporal unit constant. In general, if you move or break the temporary unit, you change the scene. An exception to this rule would be, for example, a street chase in which the space unit is broken without changing the scene. The term can also be defined as a dramatic action that could be recorded in a single plane; from this point of view, the scene would change when inescapably a cut had to be made. The fundamental objective of each scene in the classic structure script is to make history progress.

54. Linear structure: Development of a character, presentation and eventual transformation of his personality through the course of a script or argument.

55. Structure: order and form in which what happens in a story is presented. It is considered the skeleton of the script, which in traditional film history is adjusted to a first act of approach with a key incident or trigger, a second act of development usually ending in crisis, and an act of outcome with a climax and resolution, being the protagonist the epicenter of history.

56. **Study:** Filming building funded by large production companies for indoor filming that recreates both indoor and outdoor to control specific visual or mechanical effects such as chromakey (green screen), flying in the air, floods, snow, fog, etc. .

57. **F.G.:** Direction indication of a script that means Foreground, indicates everything that should be closer to the camera within an opening plane.

58. Fade in: After the cover of a script, are the words with which a script begins.

59. Fade out: After the culmination of a script, are the words with which a script ends.

60. Flashbacks: One or several scenes that interrupt the normal narrative thread of the script to show events that occurred at a point in the past.

61. Flashforwards: One or several scenes that interrupt the normal narrative thread of the script to show events that will occur at a point in the future.

62. Format: Canon or script standard designed to facilitate the calculations of each preproduction department. Its fundamental characteristics are as follows: headings, action descriptions, dialogs and character dimensioning are made across the page in specific margins, and the dialogues are located in the center of the page in wide margins and preceded by the name of the character that speaks (in the previous line) written in capital letters and with margin almost in the center of the page; the typing is to a space, except in the passage from dialogues to description, which has double space, and in the step to a new scene or sequence, which has three spaces; the titles of the scenes or headings are capitalized. The standard script format is written in Courier 12 or Courier New 12 and it is calculated that each script page corresponds to a minute of film.

63. Initial Hook: First scene in a script needed to catalyze the main action relative to the whole concept of the script's argument.

64. Turn: unexpected change of direction in the plot marked by an unexpected event whose essential objective is to intensify the interest of the public in history.

65. Reading script: This is the format in which the script must be assigned to a production company. This should not contain numbers of scenes or visual directions and should preferably be 120 pages.

66. Filming script: written document that, in addition to the script, adds the numbers of scenes, dialogues and visual directions for photography during filming.

67. Literary script: Screenplay written by the screenwriter. The literary script must not include types of plans other camera indications, since these will be added later in the preparation of the technical script. In some countries, such as Spain, numbering is usually included as opposed to others such as the USA, where it is not usual.

68. Technical script: Script that has been incorporated a number of scenes, another column with the types of planes to use in each of them. Also it is customary to include the estimation of shooting time and indication of special effects. The director rolls the film from this script.

69. Script: A document written in a cinematographic format for the production of a 30-page short film, a 60-page medium-length film or a 90- to 120-page full-length film.

70. Screenwriter: refers to the person who writes a script. The writers can be divided into scriptwriters, biblistas, escaletistas, dialogues, depending on whether they dedicate themselves to any of the parts of the writing process of a script. We can also talk about original adapters and scriptwriters. Of all the creatives of the audiovisual work, the original screenwriter is the only one who faces nothing, and therefore, the most important figure in the creative process.

71. Screenwriter: A writer who writes scripts or original scripts, adapts them, rewrites them for cinema.

72. Identification of credits: mandatory entry on the cover of a script that indicates authorship, such as "written by:" "original story by:" "adaptation by:"

73. idiolect: the way a character uses the language. The idiolect depends on a series of variables such as vocabulary, syntax, use of jargon or slang, rhythm when speaking and all those that make up the peculiarities that should distinguish speech between different characters.

74. Indie: Anglo-Saxon term to refer to a product made independently or legal obligations imposed by a transnational producer, ie a small producer company.

75. Production Manager: is the licensed head who actively exercises control over the management of all project activities, depending on the hierarchical magnitude of the project. The percentage of fees on the bulk of profits you can get is 15%.

76. Feature film: film or film whose maximum duration is more than 60 minutes.

77. Libretista: is the scriptwriter and writer who writes series or films for television.

78. Location: Real location, specially selected for the dramatic action, situation or event. It must be outdoors and with a previous signature or filming permit agreement. When the location is part of a larger set, the larger set is first set and then the smaller set.

79. Light: type of lighting that the script indicates that there is outside while the scene is running, as opposed to other types of alternative. They are usually divided into: DAY, NIGHT, DAWN or DUSK, the first two being the most common. In the script, the scene header is indicated, in capital letters, after the location and preceded by one or two hyphens, it is reflected in the header both if we are outside and inside.

80. McGuffin: term created by Alfred Hitchcock to describe the element of dramatic curiosity, formed by some subject or object that has disappeared or that is highly desired, but to put certain stories in motion especially suspense, but which often remains relegated to a mere pretext to develop other dramatic content of greater importance, usually emotional.

81. Assembly: Final editing of the scenes using digital or analogue technique with a precise succession of images and sound.

82. Obstacles: Are all the actions, characters, and contrary decisions of the protagonist that create conflict in the story.

83. Offer: Voluntary delivery of a script to an external professional to an agency, producer, lawyer, producer, etc. However, most companies adopt the policy of rejecting unsolicited works. The best thing is to adapt to the screenwriters contests bases.

84. Option to sale: When a company or individual requests a script, they obtain the exclusive rights to produce the script within a specific period of time, which is usually one year. The contract or permit will specify the percentage charge to be paid or the sale price of the script.

85. Epic film: a genre frequently of historical context that requires immense production.

86. Pitch: It is a talk by a producer where he exposes the basic premise of his story destined to convince the listeners to request or buy his film.

87. Extreme closed plane: Close up, is when the frame of the camera emphasizes the face of the actor or an object.

88. Approach: name given to the first act of the classical structure, which lasts approximately 25% of the story and is characterized by presenting the environment and main features of the protagonist, introducing the trigger or key incident that will give rise to the History, and establish the dramatic goal and the dramatic issue, its primary functions are to know what the story is about and who is the protagonist. Create empathy towards him, to instill curiosity.

89. Premise: It is the basic concept on which history is constructed. Most of the premises can be reduced to "character X immersed in a situation and wants to get Z".

90. Premise: The basis of the idea for a story in its simplest way.

91. Financial Budget: Detailed plan of each cost or expense that will involve the filming of an audiovisual, on the line (before) or under line (post production). Usually done in a spreadsheet and under an accounting numbering standard.

92. Producer: Is the person in charge of all matters related to the production of a script, except for the creative work of the director.

Typically, it involves finding materials, arranging financing, hiring staff, and making distribution agreements.

93. Polishing: Not as drastic as rewriting, but it involves minor changes in the dialogues, narration or actions within the script.

94. Collection: The profits obtained from sales of movie theaters, video rentals, DVD sales and merchandise derived.

95. Work Registry: Means protecting the script by sending a printed or digital copy of the script to the government entity in charge to back a timely certification in case of any legal dispute.

96. Remake: It is the realization by permission of a film already released years ago, but with a new artistic focus, as well as its digital quality. It is not precisely a sequel, but an adaptation of a screenplay already shot and rededicated. Example: Titanic, Spider Man.

97. Proofreader report: document generated by a professional involved in the evaluation of a script for a potential purchase or transfer of production rights, may be final, as a suggestion or simple opinion.

98. Rhythm: cadence between the scenes and planes of a film based on the length of each other, added to the effect provoked by the information that is provided in the scenes and that makes the story progress. Rhythm is a key factor in the way the public will perceive the film.

99. Sequence: set of scenes that form a nucleus or unit of action. A sequence has its own structure, with establishment, development and outcome, containing one or more scenes that can change location or temporality, but maintaining the common bond that unites them.

100. Set or Plató: Scenography or decorative montage composed especially for the dramatic action, situation or event. It should be inside a television studio usually.

101. Synopsis of sale: synopsis whose main function is not the plot summary but the interest to awaken a second part to acquire the work. For this, the third act is not closed and enigmas are left open to interest partners in a further development of the concept.

102. Synopsis: Argument written in one to three pages that summarizes the complete structure of the story.

103. Synopsis: Brief description or summary of the topic and argument that the film deals with. With an extension of one to four pages, it is written in the present tense, with concise language and without dialogues. Includes the outcome.

104. Synthesis: Short description of the plot of the script, written in three to five lines of a paragraph, which focuses on the concept but does not give the end of it.

105. Script software: software created to help the scriptwriter in his tasks of formatting and construction of scripts.

106. Subframe: Are the actions and conflicts produced by the secondary characters that surround the central plot of the protagonists, so that according to the dramatic format, there may be more than one.

107. Fasteners: metallic piece that is used to hold wads of copies of the script, shooting plan, call sheets, etc. that should be managed by audiovisual directors.

108. Super Text: It is a layer or image that is displayed over another, most commonly used when the titles overlap the opening scene.

109. Talent: informal term to refer to the actors. Usually, an action tutoring is offered on each individual or group scene before filming.

110. Scene Cards: A method by which a scriptwriter describes each scene separately and then accommodates them at will in order to find the best option by reordering the final structure of the script.

111. Theme: central idea on which history is concerned. It is the essential stuff of a script.

112. Tempo: cadence of a scene determined by its level of activity within it, unlike the rhythm, which is determined by its overall length and its planes. Tempo is often confused with rhythm, and often a term is used to refer to the concept expressed by the other.

113. Tone: specific character of the expression or style of a story, consequence of the focus, atmosphere or climate that is printed on it.

114. Contract work: A scriptwriter is hired to take a writing assignment in exchange for an offer of payment, sometimes there is an argument in advance to be converted into a film, it is a literary adaptation with legal permission, or it is write a script that lacks professionalism. The rights will belong to the main producer or principal investor.

115. Teaser: A clip of short duration tested and shot during the development of an audiovisual project and used to demonstrate the visual concept in an introductory way, regardless of whether this will be done or not.

116. Trailer: Promotional commercial of a film that is used as a marketing technique before the premiere of a movie in theaters, Internet, radio and television.

117. Spoiler: dirty and subliminal propaganda to discredit a person, ideology or movement.

118. Plot: set of events chained to each other to advance the story and finally bring it to its conclusion.

119. Transition: It is the action of moving from one scene to the next. Transitions can be made directly, through a cut, or they can be made through a certain effect. The scriptwriter occasionally chooses a type of transition to denote an abstract idea.

120. Sequenced treatment: Detailed treatment and with the scene headers. It's practically a script without dialogues.

121. Treatment: It is longer than a short synopsis, with all the dramatic turns counted in the present tense: Juan is ... Juan walks by ..., etc.

122. Vocal: term to differentiate the dialogue pronounced by the character from the voiceovers. The voices or dialogue in off can express thought of the personages, narration, dialogues pronounced outside picture box or in contiguous spaces, electronic or mechanical voices like the own ones of the telephone or radios, and another type of superimposed voices. Although the Spanish-speaking countries maintain the English origin of several of these as OS., V.O, etc.

Bibliography

BOOKS :

* Film director. FELDMAN, Simon.
* Realistic genres in television: Reality shows.
* Production of Programs. KAPLÚN, M.
* The Tools of Screenwriting. HOWARD, David and MABLEY, Edward.
* Adventures in the Screen Trade. GOLDMAN, William.
* The complete Guide to standard Script formats. COLE, JR., Hillis and HAAG, Judith.
* Screenwriting Business. WRIGHT, Leonore and BOND, Angela.
* Selected works in six lathes. EISENTEN, Sergei. Volume 2. Editions "Art" Moscow "The Cinematographic Effigy". Andrei Tarkovskij
* Fundamentals of Cinematography. O.F. NECHAY and G_V. RAANIKOOV, Editions The Art of Cinema Second edition. Edited by the Ministry of Middle and Higher Education of Belarus.
* The Language of Cinema.
* The Sense of Cinema. EISENTEN, Sergei. Editions of the Department of Cultural Activities. University of the Haban, series Literature and Art.
* Television Producing and directing. BLUMENTHAL, H. 1987.
* Dictionary of Broadcast Communications. DIAMANT, L., 1991.

ENCYCLOPEDIAS:

* Encyclopedia Encarta. Microsoft Corporation. 2006
* Wikipedia.com

DICTIONARIES:

* Oceano Dictionary of Synonyms and Antonyms. Editorial Ocean. Barcelona, Spain.
* Spanish dictionary. Royal Spanish Academy. Twenty-first edition. Volume I and II. Madrid Spain. 1992

INTERNET PAGES:

* http://amodelsdiary.blogspot.com Castings Calls
* www.backstage.com 10 tips for winning Audition.
* "The cinema in definitions", by Valentin Fernandez - Tubau Rodés, Director of the Technical Area and Services of abcguionistas.com

MONOGRAPHS, MAGAZINES AND OTHER SOURCES:

* Notes "Film Workshop, Public Mind". Several teachers Panama, 2015.
* Notes "Panama Film Lab". Several international exponents. Panama, 2013
* Workshops "Writing a script", International Film Festival of Panama. Panama, 2014.
* Apuntes, "Radio and television production", University of Panama. 2003

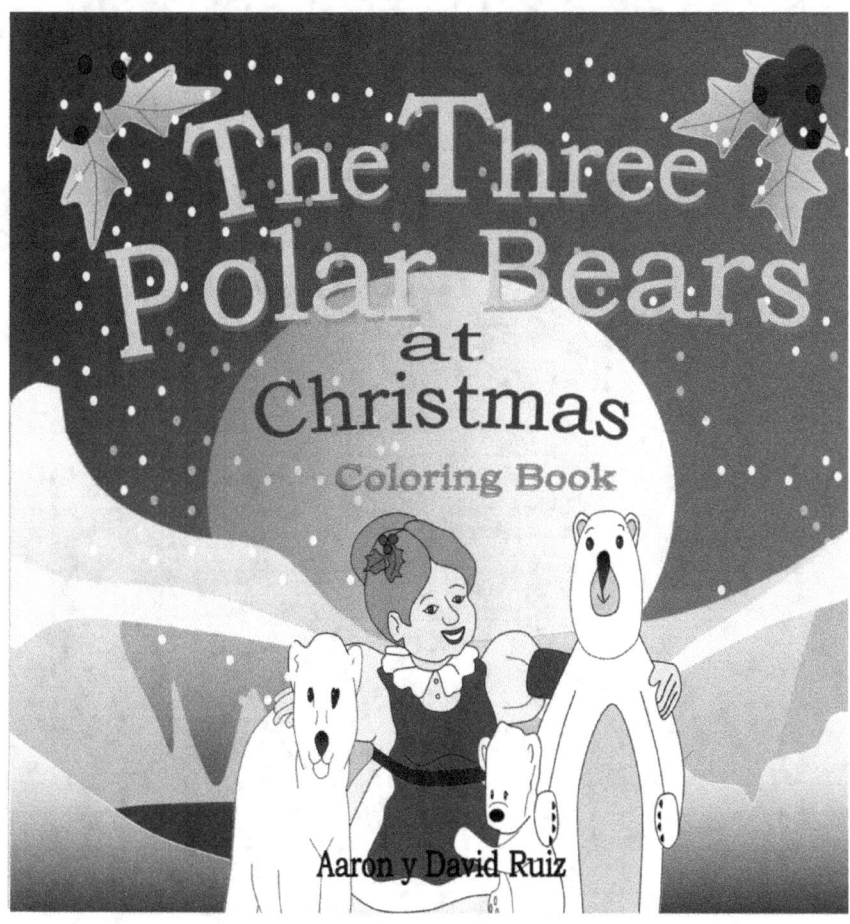

For more information on these books, visit the page with the complete list, we suggest you consult our author page in the following electronic link:
amazon.com/author/mykindlebooks

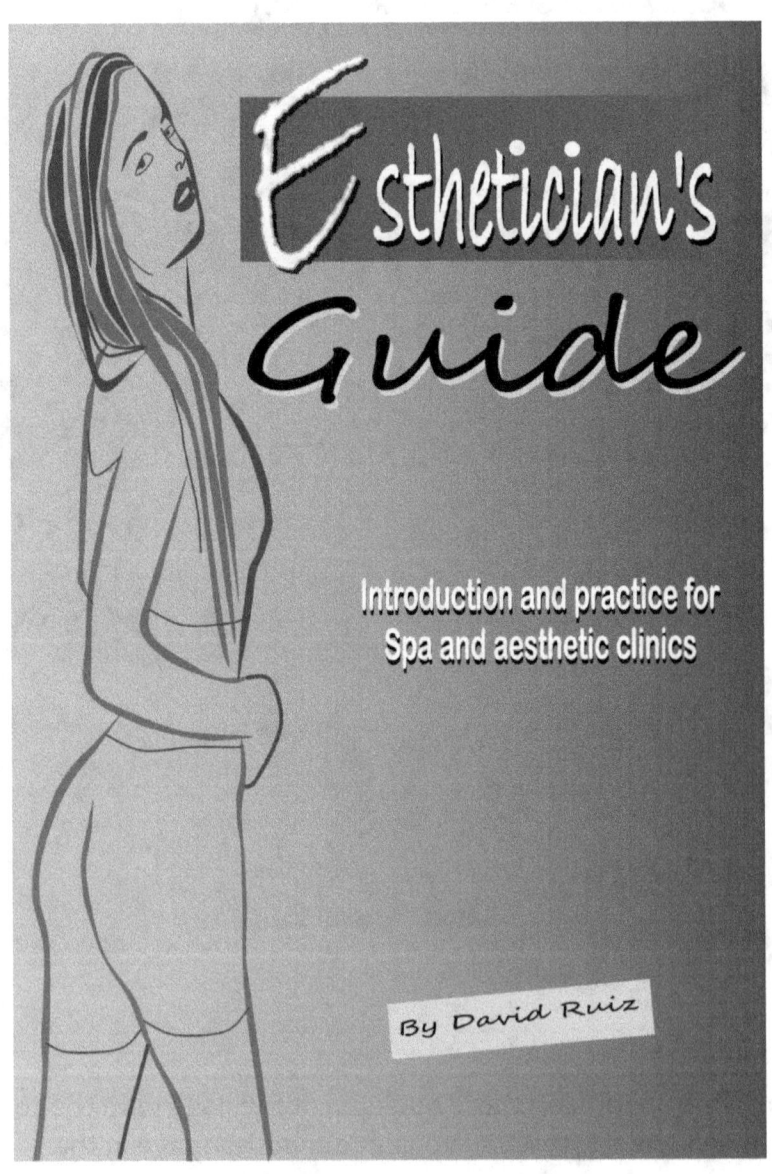

Esthetician's Guide

Introduction and practice for
Spa and aesthetic clinics

By David Ruiz

For more information on these books, visit the page with the complete
list, we suggest you consult our author page in the
following electronic link:
amazon.com/author/mykindlebooks

Servicios Promonet

Promoting knowledge on the Internet

www.ingramcontent.com/pod-product-compliance
Lightning Source LLC
Chambersburg PA
CBHW071448220526
45472CB00003B/717